CHAL[illegible]G RACISM

All London Teachers Against Racism & Fascism
(A.L.T.A.R.F.)

ISBN 0 9509673 0 0 1984

Typeset by Terri D'Silva, 38 Mount Pleasant, London WC1X 0AP
Printed by the Russell Press, Gamble Street, Nottingham
Distributed by ALTARF, Room 216, Panther House, 38 Mount Pleasant, London WC1X 0AP

ALTARF is grant aided by the Greater London Council

Cover photo by Anna Sherwin

CONTENTS

This book is dedicated to the Newham 8
and the children of
William Patten Infant and Junior Schools
and all young people who are
struggling against racism.

INTRODUCTION

Since its formation in 1978, ALTARF has been involved in the struggle against state racism and has campaigned for LEAs and schools to pursue effective anti-racist policies. These years have witnessed the growing acceptance by LEAs of a bland and totally de-politicised form of multi-cultural education alongside the intensification of state racism in the form of ever increasing deportations, police brutality against Black people, discrimination in employment and harassment in unemployment.

Black people continue to be in the forefront of this kind of state oppression and continue to lead the resistance to it. Increasingly, and rapidly, other groups are being subjected to the same kind of oppression and beginning to organise similar resistance. Greenham Common women, the NGA and the NUM provide recent examples of specific abuses by the state, of democratic rights which we had thought inviolate. Teachers who have traditionally felt that such matters as these are outside their 'non-political' brief are being forced to think again as they see their own position threatened by the abolition of local democracy and the effects of the government's rate capping proposals.

Challenging Racism attempts to extend the thinking behind effective anti-racist teaching and to outline strategies to implement it. Inevitably, our thinking about anti-racism has developed and continues to develop as we hope this book shows. While we have not attempted in this book to deal with issues of class and gender or to consider what some see as their apparent contradictions, in our classroom practice, individuals among us are exploring these issues and seeing them as inextricably linked to anti-racist teaching.

In *Challenging Racism* we look at matters which concern all involved in education and in so doing hope to contribute to the breaking down of barriers between primary and secondary education and between separate subject areas. We see too the need for collaborative work between parents, children and teachers and the importance and value of sharing experiences and ideas.

We do not see the school as isolated from the community. Anti-racist teaching which stops at the classroom door cannot truly be described as anti-racist. We must challenge inside and outside the school, the racism, sexism and class structures which divide us.

Altarf Collective, June 1984

RACISM AND EDUCATION

Jane Shallice

INTRODUCTION

This article is a written version of a talk given by the author in May 1983 to introduce a course on anti-racist education. Although the talk was given some time ago we have included it because it raises important issues that form a background to the rest of the book.

Racism as it presently exists and functions is assumed by many people in schools and in education to be timeless and 'known': but we must be aware of such simplistic and wrong assessments of the phenomenon with which we are dealing. Racism is not an unchanging social feature but it is derived from and tied to specific cultural, political and social forms of the societies in which it is present. We need only look at the last one hundred years in Britain to see that the forms in which racism is manifested have changed. During the mid-nineteenth century, the ideology of white superiority was unchallenged; culturally obvious and reinforced by the might of Empire, the missioning of Christianity and the building of Britain on the backs of the colonized. This white dominance and superiority was 'proved' at every turn as, with the flowering of the natural sciences in the later part of the nineteenth century, proof was evident in every classification and research that was developed. "The resulting intellectual tensions were resolved after 1859 by a comprehensive evolutionism which was at once monogeist and racist, affirmed human unity even as it relegated the dark-skinned savage to a status very near the ape." (S. J. Gould, *The Mismeasure of Man.*) Ethnographers and anthropologists measuring cranial length and width, length of arm and leg, pelvic size, weight, height and bodily function produced a fine hierarchy of 'racial types' – the apogee being the white Anglo-Saxon Protestant male. (The exhibition at the Natural History Museum developed in the 1960s on Human Evolution still produced the *white* male (dominant posture) and *white* female (submissive posture) as the figures which were the nadir of evolutionary development.)

In the early part of this century with developments in the areas of quantification of intelligence, the correlations between race and IQ were reflecting the known racial hierarchies. The white race was 'known' to be culturally, physically, morally and genetically superior – and the rest were littered back down the ladder.

In the development of evolutionary theories, racism underpinned the interpretation of evidence which was produced, whether, as in the late nineteenth century, scientists were arguing that recapitulation theory demonstrated black people were inferior to white because they retained 'juvenile physical traits' or when this theory was subsequently discussed and the reverse interpretation of evolution became accepted – that of neoteny – human evolution entailing the retention of previous juvenile features. It may be assumed that this reversal would 'prove' a superiority of black, but no luck – scientists rejected the evidence previously used and took factors to support the superiority of the white race yet again. That was racism. And although there is still much of this baggage remaining, it is seldom theorised and expounded in quite this way. There are still the spin offs from the Race/IQ debate as with the

Jensenites but substantially this is not part of the acknowledged present. A new racist ideology has developed, which is no less dangerous in its effects, again based on scientific 'theory' and couched in commonsense terms. It is now being argued that racism is part of Human Nature. The present racist statements do not address themselves openly to racial hierarchies, but to differences. The argument now presented goes along the lines that whites are not superior to blacks but they are different and as such cannot be expected to exist without asserting the importance of that difference and the impossibility of it being otherwise. One '....... finds that an absence of classificatory racism is turned into a virtue and used to conceal very real motivational *racism* that tells people that it is only natural to meet strangers with hostility." (M Barker.) Enoch Powell on BBC 9th June 1969 stated 'An instinct to preserve an identity and defend a territory is one of the deepest and strongest implanted in mankind. I happen to believe that the instinct is good and that its beneficial effects are not exhausted."

The argument now being made states that it is natural and good to form a bonded community; natural to live in a nation separate from and aware of its differences from other nations; natural to be different and inalienably separate from other cultures. In the conventional wisdom of the New Right, human nature appears to be the key to the world.

Present day Tory ideology contains this message from Thatcher's 'swamping' speech, to the Falklands messages about 'the nation', 'our folk', 'the stand of all the people': the deep seated 'knowledge' of the homogeneity of the nation, the danger or fear and hostility of different new and dynamic cultures. Powell's speeches of '68 and after were only the forerunners, the followers began to use the theories of the sociobiologists Dawkins, Wilson and Michael Ruse and the popularization of the behaviourists, Lorenz, Morris and Ardrey. Their writings theorised the 'tendency to form distinct groups and feel different, real deep down different, from members of other groups' (Martin Barker, *New Racism*) and it was just what was needed. Ardrey wrote of 'nation-forming', Lorenz 'pseudo-speciation', Morris stated, 'I am not arguing that there can be world-wide brotherhood of man. That is a naive utopian dream. Man is a tribal animal and the great super tribes will always be in competition with each other', Wilson that, 'Nationalism and racism to take two examples, are the culturally nurtured outgrowths of simple tribalism'. And in the words of Martin Barker's response, 'And they (the sociobiologists and behaviourists) all agree that simple tribalism (whatever that may be) is just kin altruism in action. It's just an extension of loving your family.'

The use of biological theories to justify and 'prove' social and political ideologies is not of course new, and its acceptance is based on the premise that science is ideologically neutral and is *objective.* It denies the position that scientists will look at the world as 'scientists' but through the spectacles of their social position. Dawkins, one of sociobiology's gurus, claims that his science is above mere human politics: his work and theories about genetic material underpin the world of human activity and any understanding of human activity is totally dependant on accepting that the genetic makeup of individuals will be the key to their social responses. The collective is seen only as the summation of individuals, no more or less, and in the research being done on locating brain areas and cell processes that manifest agression, it is argued that we can understand why societies are 'aggressive' because they are formed from individuals with these genetically determined responses! Fascists have not been slow in responding to this new 'evidence' for the corrections of their racism – Verall has proudly proclaimed that 'Racism is the product of our selfish genes.'

Whose world is the world? *Poster Film Collective BCM PFC, London WC1*

As uncritical neo-Darwinists, the sociobiologists expounded the 'survival of the fittest' and argued from theories of adaption that genes and/or biology have given us the best of all possible worlds. All that is needed is to find the properties of genes, accept the premise of human nature, assume key concepts of survival and adaptation and then accept all that has happened as 'inevitable' and/or 'determined'.

In opposition to such theories we cannot reject biology and say that it is irrelevant but we can and must argue that we are *active participants* in the environment not passive recipients: that our genotypes are *not* the sole way that we relate to the world.

But racism is a *structural* feature of our society, it is not beliefs or ideas floating in the air but beliefs and ideas that are being constructed and sustained by practices and operations of the society in which we live. Created and maintained through relationships based on domination and subordination: racism is not the product of prejudice but of *power*. As an ideology it is a set of beliefs and ways of structuring lives which are rooted in material existences. And it is the reality of these existences which entrenches and deepens the manifestation of racism, which reveal a character appearing to be resistant to attempts at reform. Racism is not reducible therefore to a simple ideological phenomenon and has to be located within the structures and relations of British society, conditioned centrally by the historical development of capitalism. The complex amalgam of factors and circumstances provides a framework within which racism can be analysed but it is also intermeshed with the current endogenous political forces – racism being recreated and reinterpreted by the political forces – racism being recreated and reinterpreted by the politics of Britain and within Britain over the last thirty to forty years. As Hall states *now* it is racism 'at home', before then it was largely 'abroad': and the present manifestations of racism are

are in part the product of Britain's decline. Previously it was a character of an expanding social formation. Over the period since 1945 with the need for capital to suck into the metropolitan countries a large labour force – Britain's black population increased, becoming in the mordant comment of Castles and Kosacks 'a form of aid given by the poor countries to the rich'. There appear to have been three broad phases in state relations to the black population: an encouragement for Black entry up until the '62 Act: a period through the 60's and early 70's of policy packages produced to deal with 'problems': and through the last ten years the development of a form of policy proposals which verge upon crisis management – the increasing hard cop/soft cop tactics of control and containment – increasing police powers plus injections of money into urban and community projects and 'boulevards' for 'Toxteth' or 'leisure centres for Hackney'. The last ten years have elicited this state response as the British economy and policy have been faced by an increasingly severe crisis. With the end of welfarism, the lack of a solution to the decline of Britain's economic stance, the consensus between both Tory and Labour Governments attacks on public expenditure; the Tory response developing a cavalier attitude to increasing unemployment and an assumption of neo-conservative economic and social policies since 1979, has increased the pressures on the black communities and constantly the focus of scrutiny is being directed away from the economic crisis and being targetted upon the social and political sphere. 'The symptoms of our malaise may be economic, may show themselves in price rises, shortages and industrial disputes, but underlying the symptoms is a disease which has destroyed democracies in the past and the causes of that disease are not economic, they are moral and political and constitutional, and in order to cure it we must recognise them as such', Lord Hailsham. This certainly is underpinned by the new

Immigration Regulations and Nationality Act which are redefining precisely who is British i.e. who is part of the corpus and who is really outside. In the 1970's Clutterbuck floated views on the breakdown of law and order, 'the enemy within' – youth, Unions and blacks: and over the last fifteen years 'law and order' is a central issue for the Tory party. Since 1979 through immigration legislation and nationality law the state is therefore redefining who precisely is British. 'The imposition of mass immigration from backward alien cultures is just one symptom of this self-destructive urge reflected in the assault on patriotism, the family – both as a conjugal and economic unity – the Christian religion in public life and schools, traditional morality in matters of sex, honest, public display and respect for the law – in short all that is English and wholesome.'

And where are we in Education?

The educational response through the 1960's was one of an assimilationist model, the DES wanting 'successful assimilation of immigrant children' – the problem was seen as black pupils *not* racism or the white response. Where there were 'concentrations' of more than 30% black pupils in schools those black children had to be bussed to areas away from their homes. Assimilation being designed to protect the indigenous white population. One headteacher quoted in Brittain and Townsend, 'Continuous discussion of racial differences in culture and tradition seems to perpetuate them. I do not consider it the responsibility of an English State School to cater for the development of cultures and customs of a foreign nature, I believe our duty is to prepare children for citizenship in a free Christian democratic society according to British standards and customs.'

By the 1970s dispersal policies were being attacked as in Haringey, and abandoned; Coard had raised the issues of black children being identified and 'treated' as ESN and from Roy Jenkins were coming strictures about integration – unity through cultural diversity (he of the Immigration Acts of late 60's!). Special needs budgets were devised – special problems needing special treatment, by special teachers, black pupils = special education.

But throughout this period, pious hopes were ignoring concrete realities: black groups in Britain did not and do not enjoy equality. Gus John's statement was an apposite comment on the position that many black people were coming to articulate: 'To wish to integrate with that which alienates and destroys you, rendering you less than a person is madness. To accept the challenge to join it and change it from within, when it refuses to accept that you are there in in your fullness and refuses to acknowledge the results of interaction between you and it, is double madness.'

Racism is not merely individual ignorance, it is intimately enmeshed in institutional forms and social practices and it will require more than the 'education for cultural diversity.'

So what now?

Anti-Racism in Education

As teachers we need to define what is racist and to recognise the manifestations of it: it also requires that we have to work out precisely in what ways we confront it. In our role as teachers, we are concerned with the development and formation of intellectual ideas and as such we are in a very different relationship to our work than, for example, car workers. As 'intellectual workers' or 'ideological workers' we have a responsibility to expose the illusions of racism, to engage in that fight against it and if we are not prepared to do this, we end up as agents in its perpetuation. We cannot take a neutral stance.

There are still overt acts of racism in schools, in all

sectors of education, and we cannot cower away from tackling them, and yet in no way can one underestimate the enormity of this task. One crucial area which needs to be asserted with no hesitation, is that of supporting black teachers and pupils exposed to racist abuse or attacks either from pupils or from staff; and supporting them when facing these situations. Responses in school must be immediate and collective, but where this is not possible, must then be individual. This may appear to be so obvious that it may seem not to be worth stating but the institutional protection developed to glide over dealing with overt acts of racism has been well tried. It is not just necessary to identify such acts, it does mean that there has often to be a real fight to have such situations dealt with to the satisfaction of black people who have been involved.

However, it is also evident that there have been major developments in anti-racist education over the last few years – the most important being the increasing presence of the black voice, presenting demands of the black community, particularly on educational issues. Of increasing importance is the demand that the institutional racist practices be analysed and addressed – and in education this means that the recruitment and promotion of black teachers is now a central issue. The particular economic and political climate in which we are now working, may not seem favourable for the raising of such issues, but in no way can it be avoided. The black community is now demanding the accountability of a system, which proclaims itself to be anti-racist. Therefore the pivotal issue of the equality in employment may be seen as the marker of precisely how adequate is the response.

There are other demands from sections of the black community, which also present teachers with the need to respond to issues that the black community places as high priority. In some areas, the demand for mother tongue teaching as part of the mainstream curriculum is increasingly important, and although in some authorities gestures towards the pressure have been made, there are few examples of schools that have made responses other than as an added extra, after school or squeezed into some corner of the timetable. But over the last two or three years, there are other issues that the black organisations have been centrally involved in, which again have to be acknowledged by teachers; acknowledged and supported. This has been especially around issues of Immigration and Nationality law, and the relationship of the black community to the police. These are not issues that can be 'relegated' to the outside of school for they are the basis of the racist underpinnings of the state; and as such present the real face of British society to the black community. Deportations of families or individuals undermine the black presence in Britain – and teachers have to participate actively in the campaigns.

Finally, what is it that we as teachers can do within the classroom? If it is accepted that teachers are seen to be taking up and participating within the fight against racism in both is institutional and its overt forms, it is also necessary to consider what we are teaching. Racism will not be eradicated through exemplary curricular practice, but it is possible that teachers can begin to deconstruct the obvious and to present a framework within which there is an increased knowledge of the issues involved – Colonialism and imperialism seen as key determinants of the present racism evident within Britain, a critical understanding of the society, the relationship between the social context, the economic and political and the cultural manifestations of struggle. Stuart Hall posed the problems and sketched out the areas of a solution in his article *Teaching Race* (NAME Vol.9 No.1).

'Somehow one has to steer that difficult line while not selling short the complexity of the issues with which you are dealing. Instead of thinking that the questions of race are some sort of moral duty, moral intellectual academic duty which white people with good feelings do for black, one has to remember that the issues of race provides one of the most important ways of understanding how this society actually works and how it has arrived where it is. It is one of the most important keys not into the margins of society, but right into its dynamic centre. It is a very good way of getting into the political and social issues of contemporary Britain, because it touches and connects with so many facets. That does make it a difficult problem to handle and to explain adequately and one mustn't go for simple explanations because one does want to create a dynamic which involves people in trying to build anti-racist politics.'

INSTITUTIONAL RACISM : LEA ACTION NEEDED

Betty Hunter

In the winter 1983 edition of *The Head Teachers Review*, a CRE officer writes of "the existence of institutionalised racism as a major obstacle in coming face to face with the needs of the black community and young black people in particular". He argues that the practice of schools is a part of that institutionalised racism and that this must be an area for radical change. But will the headteachers understand what is meant by institutionalised racism, and more crucially, do the LEAs in the increasing numbers of anti-racist policy documents understand the need to tackle institutionalised racism?

Society creates institutions to serve and perpetuate its needs. The relationship between the institutions and society is a fluid one. But essentially, our schools operate fundamentally from an ethos that a few students will succeed but the majority will fail. Race, sex and class operate within that ethos as the most important determining factors of success/failure. We must welcome ILEA's attempt to tackle these three factors in the schools, and support them. But that support can only be positive if we maintain that change cannot come from the schools alone but in conjunction with the wider community. And if the wider community is to be meaningfully involved in the changes we seek for our students, then ILEA must begin to give students, parents, black and community groups the rights to know, understand and question the everyday work of the schools. Teacher attitudes will only broaden in the open atmosphere of accountability.

During this academic year teachers and schools in London have been instructed to review their attitudes and policies on race. But just how far is the ILEA prepared to go? The danger is that by focusing on the individual teacher's attitudes, the schools as institutions reflecting and perpetuating the racism of society will remain outside of or above the debate while the overworked teachers may become pressurised by what seems yet another demand from an out of touch employer.

As the prologue to the discussion on anti-racist and multi-ethnic education, the ILEA presented us with document 1 : *Achievement in Schools.* The aim is, of course, to improve the achievements of students by looking at the practice of schools and why students fail, but is it good enough to say, "The view of many is that public examinations should be less concerned with 'who is best' but with ensuring that as many pupils as possible reach the educational standards required for successful lives in our society."?

Yes, be critical of the examination system, yes, try to change the system, yes, try to promote alternative learning situations, but always in the knowledge that until we eradicate the oppression of blacks, women and the working class from our society, it is not possible to provide equality of opportunity in schools. Yet we must be active in supporting the pressure for change.

The students, their parents and we, their teachers, know that society requires from the educational system a method of selecting out a few people to succeed. Whether or not we continue to use public examinations, or the new 'profile' system of assessment, graded assessments, or the next educational camouflage, we will be expected to help construct the social pyramid. This does not make the debate about method totally irrelevant, but it does require that we are fully conscious of the terms of the debate so that we engage in it positively with our own anti-racist framework.

Failure is built into our education system but if we look at the position of black youth, the failure of schools is more consistent and proportionately higher than for other groups. The criteria for 'successful lives in our society' can mean anything to anyone. Liberalising learning and experience in schools does not necessarily provide students with the means for exercising control over their lives, either in schools or in the future. It must be accompanied by structural change.

Achievement must continue to be seen as two sides of the educational coin, that of personal development and that of the present currency in society. To disguise the system of selection with anodyne phrases or even palatable classroom practice is not enough. All students know that they will be judged in terms of examination success. In supporting this aim, as well as that of developing independence of thought, personal control and confidence, many teachers have looked at the content of our curriculum and our teaching methods. We do see these as crucial elements in the learning process but they can only play a progressive role for the students if they are tackled in conjunction with the structures of the schools themselves.

The good practices of the classrooms remain isolated experiences which may benefit a few students and teachers but which do not affect the educational system at all, even the long-term process of osmosis would influence only a few more classrooms. This is why a real commitment from the ILEA and its teachers to looking at the schools as institutions, and the ways that their organisation reinforces and perpetuates racism is necessary.

Yet in posing one of its priority tasks as "Removing discrimination in educational establishments", the ILEA defines its arena as: presenting positive black models of experience; tackling the influence of teacher expectations in the allocation of students to streams, bands and particular courses; and ways of consulting parents and communities.

The first area is for the teachers as groups of interested people to deal with. For the past ten years many teachers have been looking at the content of lessons. We have attempted to incorporate all cultures as of equal value, we have taken up the effects of current racism on the lives and learning potential of our students, welcoming the students' contributions themselves, in these and other areas. More does need to be done, of course, but the ILEA needs to define how its schools can undertake this on a large scale, to give authoritative backing to positive input, with funding for those people undertaking the work in schools not just specialist groups, and with an inspectorate, active in disseminating good practice. Indeed, the authorities have a more immediate way of dealing with this, by positive action to employ more black teachers.

In the second area, the ILEA does admit that there may be an institutional form for racist discrimination in streaming and banding etc. But what is their solution? They simply bat the ball back into the court of individual teachers' conscious or unconscious racist attitudes, asking them to review their expectations when engaged in the process of selection and allocation. Teachers have always believed they are allocating students on sound educational grounds, it is no good exhorting them to clear themselves of racism and expecting them to engage in individual ideological change. Racism is not simply an ideology in teachers' and students' minds, in the resources and language we use, but it is materially embodied in the structure and organisation of the schools. Why do the streams, the sin bins, the non-examination classes, the 'community' courses exist if not to justify the fact that society will not offer 'successful lives' to more than a few?

The ILEA cannot ignore the situation, especially when the Tory Government laps up any means by which it can 'blame' teachers for poor educational standards.

Many schools are operating mixed ability classes. They need the support of the ILEA in developing their methods and in offering them as examples of a tangible, practical way to begin to tackle the institutionalised assumption that most of our students will fail in education, particularly if they are black. Only in this way, will the power of subjective teacher attitudes and expectations over the lives of students begin to be eroded. How else will the ILEA tackle the necessary task of challenging teacher attitudes, of raising awareness, if not by having discussions over particular educational policy? As long as the schools accept that children of different abilities need to be segregated out so that more 'appropriate' education can be offered to all groups, then the basis on which the divisions occur are open to abuse, conscious or unconscious. The education authorities should provide the means by which teachers can teach all children effectively, through small classes, with specialist help in specific educational areas. Only by giving an organisational form to the principle of equal opportunity can we begin to challenge the notion that most children don't want to learn and will not succeed. These expectations of teachers have become the expectations of the students precisely because they are reflected both in the way society allocates its resources to people and in the organisation of schools. The resources for sin bins, for remedial groups, etc., must be redirected and increased to support the work of teachers and students learning in mixed ability classrooms.

Ironically, alongside the anti-racist initiative, the ILEA is putting more resources into grading and testing on the basis of fragmented skills. Surely the educational debate on both equality of opportunity and on anti-racist education has highlighted the mis-direction of such efforts. Establishing an effective learning environment is not about testing and more testing, which emphasises failure more strongly than success, despite the hopes of education authorities.

It is not simply on the level of selection that the teacher expectations operate to label students. Much of a school's resources are put into pastoral care. But this care often takes the form of control and discipline and inevitably leads to a particular view of teachers by the students and their parents. When the students are seen as problems, their parents are invited to become involved at school level. The parents are then expected to answer for their 'problem' children and those who actually question the school and its methods become 'problem' parents.

The figures for suspensions highlight the situation in our schools, the black youth predominate, as they do in disruptive units, etc. But could we redefine 'care' away from the control model to that of caring in the teaching/learning situation? We do have difficult times in our classrooms but would we be more effective in achieving a working, educational atmosphere if we shared our aims and methods with students and parents. They might then begin to shape their aims and hopes with the caring teachers in schools.

By referring to consultation with parents and local communities the ILEA again recognises that the issue of accountability is central if we are to challenge the racism in schools. Schools as institutions have always protected themselves as being the places where experts, whose knowledge is unquestionable, feed the minds of students to capacity. The performance of each student depends entirely on their individual capacity. The only groups who have had any influence on these schools have been the middle-class parents organising to ensure that their children are given the maximum opportunity to succeed (e.g. William Tyndale School).

The language in which the school presents itself to parents is standard English. The use of mother tongue letters and notices is slowly increasing but has not yet become generalised, and the set-up for parents' evenings remains largely the teacher informing the parent of a student's progress in terms of achievement of skills. In this framework there is no real participation in education.

The schools are separate from the community, accountable to the government, education authorities, always judged on the basis of the needs of government policy as mediated through examination courses, etc. It is essential that this relationship is not allowed to continue as the only influence on the schools. But participation rather than consultation is necessary if parents and students are to be really involved.

The ILEA suggests that the involvement of the parents and community be obtained not by involvement in the educational work and policies of the school, but in being 'canvassed for their support in the development' (of the ILEA's anti-racist policy). The failure of parental involvement, particularly in secondary schools, is well known. And so long as parents are expected to listen to fairly banal comments on their children's progress and behaviour or to raise money for a school project, who can blame them for staying away? Parents are forced by teachers to believe that we know best, our professional judgement can't be questioned. Indeed, that is what we tell the students as well.

Of course we do have expertise, we are trained. But do we always know best how students learn? Particularly as anti-racist teachers, we must be prepared to explain our methods, our purpose to students and parents? If we accept that making inroads in the structure and organisation of schools is more fundamental to the fight against racism than simply looking at curriculum and method, then we must put aside our vulnerability and create a dialogue between ourselves and students and parents on educational practice and policy. How long will parents and students put up with the 'labelling' if they are actively engaged in assessing education? But equally, how long will they worry about small group talk, collaborative work, when it is presented as part of a view of education as positive action of the students in learning? And if there is to be consultation, how will it be organised? The governors of schools are clearly not representative of the community served by the schools. But to replace political appointees with those of community groups does not necessarily ensure more accountability. The governors of schools must all be actively accountable and must be representative of the community not simply specific organised interest groups.

Language is clearly the living and generative expression of all of our experience. Its part in the formation of ideology is well documented. All community languages should be recognised as important and bilingualism must certainly be viewed by schools as a skill which shows a high degree of language proficiency. Of course this means that our positive reception in schools of non-English mother-tongue is crucial. The ILEA is committed to this principle in terms of bi-lingual teaching. If this is to be the general pattern in schools, however, much work will have to be undertaken, including consultations with the non-English mother-tongue community and in-service for teachers.

It is too easy to assume that the communities want their languages taught in schools whereas some see mother-tongue teaching as the role of support and community schools, enabling independent organisation for the communities. There is a tension between the need for competent and effective English and the development of literacy and advancement in the mother-tongue languages. We know that competence and development in mother-tongue actually supports the acquisition of English. (See article by D. Medcraft.) But we need more than a simplistic response in schools to the question of relating the two. More work on the best ways of developing learning in both languages is essential, but the commitment of the schools is needed.

The record of ILEA and its schools on the use of Section II money would be an interesting area for research and an indicator of material commitment. How many schools have actually employed specialist help for second language learners and how many have used it to create smaller classes generally, or absorbed it into the pool of school resources?

Schools could seek to present non-English mother-tongue teachers in positions where they can be seen to be valued for all of their skills, as a start to the positive acceptance of bi-lingualism. We must certainly guard against these teachers merely becoming translators. And non-European languages should be made available to all students in schools as subjects worthy of study.

Indeed, if the authority is serious about tackling the issue of racism it is precisely in the area of staffing that they can show that they mean to act. In the schools the physical evidence is that black teachers are a minority, while in non-teaching staff such as cleaners, dinner ladies, there is often a higher proportion of black people. The black teachers have documented the extent to which they are subjected to institutionalised racism, in terms of promotion, career development, actual job situation in schools and in general terms their treatment by the staff and pupils in schools. We know that the number of black supernumary teachers is disproportionate, as is the number of black teachers transferred by the authority from school to school. The ILEA has got to show all of those people whom it expects to implement the anti-racist policy that as an employer they are taking positive action to redress the situation. Confidence in the authority can only be given when we feel confident that the authority will back the black teachers in fighting the real discrimination and racism they face in the schools as organised institutions.

The lead must be given by the ILEA and other education authorities in more than written documents. Those teachers prepared to be active on anti-racism in schools must be given the practical backing of the authority, the black teachers must be given evidence of the authority's commitment to positive action, and the students and parents must be given real power to participate in all of educational policy. Only then will we be able to say that having recognised the crucial area of institutionalised racism can we begin to combat it.

THE POSITION OF BLACK TEACHERS IN THIS SOCIETY

Lynette Hubah

Co-ordinator Hackney Black Teachers Group and Inner London Black Teachers Group; member of the National Convention of Black Teachers.

This critique of the position of Black teachers in this society is illustrated by reference to some (a few among hundreds) of the experiences and complaints compiled by Black organisations. The views expressed are my own. They have grown out of many years teaching in this country, years of attending courses, seminars and conferences. These have been years during which I have been observant, concerned and highly disillusioned by the progress – or rather lack of it – that Black teachers have been allowed to make in this country. The position of the Black teacher is constantly put under review by the powers that be. The pressure brought to bear on all teachers is made worse for Black teachers by the added pressure of racism. Black teachers are made to feel as if they are perpetually under a magnifying glass.

We hope that in this year of the GLC Anti-Racist Campaign people will become more aware of racism in society – overt and covert racism; personal and institutional racism – and that the situation will improve. But doubts remain. We do not know how receptive minds will be to the overall changes which the whole of society has to undergo. We do not know how people will view the consequences of these changes. Only time can tell, but if individuals concertedly make a positive and constructive effort to eradicate the miscarriages of justice that have been inflicted on Black and Ethnic minority people through the years, then and only then, can we say that 'this has been a battle well fought and truly won'. Mere awareness alone cannot achieve anything. Positive and constructive effort from everyone is the only remedy.

The Position of Black Teachers

The term 'Black' is used extensively in our society to classify all non-white ethnic groups, as opposed to classifying in terms of racial stereotypes. It may refer to the culture or way of life of a group as much as to physical characteristics. 'Black' refers to those arguments beliefs and practices which serve to identify and set apart minority groups on the basis of their particular characteristics – racial, cultural and so on – which are all negatively valued in this racist society. 'Black' is currently used as a term to denote a unity of origins and a state of consciousness applicable to all oppressed, non-white people who have settled in this country.

This does not mean that there is universal agreement among the Black community about the use of the term 'Black'. One example of this discrepancy is that some Asians do not see themselves, or are not acknowledged by others, as Black. The term Asian itself is a misnomer – but one has to beware of such arguments and not be carried away by the complex semantics of the term Black. The main point here is that to White Anglo-Saxon people, our precise origins don't matter. They regard us as Black and for them the term has negative connotations. Even when we are from a family which has been in this country for hundreds of years we are classified as Black rather than as British. Even if one of our parents is White we are still seen (negatively) as Black.

It is therefore, vital that we are consistent and definite about the term used in our struggle against oppression. 'Black' is the positive term by which all settlers from Third World countries and their descendants will be collectively known. Where appropriate, national and ethnic origins can be further identified for clarity.

The ILEA in its documents *Race, Sex and Class* use the terms 'Afro-Caribbean' and 'Asian' as well as 'Black' in an attempt to clarify the ethnic groups from which our school population is drawn. But this is a feeble attempt to classify people of such diversity. The term 'Afro-Caribbean' is used to refer to all people whose origins are in Africa or the Caribbean. This term is now widely mis-used to classify one kind of people – Caribbean people of African descent. The other ethnic groups of the Caribbean are rarely mentioned and it is increasingly becoming accepted as if fact that the only inhabitants of the Caribbean are the people of African descent.

Such terminology should not be mis-used and should not be the criteria by which one group can laud it over another and get preference when applying for jobs. Sociological factors and political considerations are resulting in a high amount of positive discrimination being applied to certain groups to the disadvantage of other ethnic minority groups. This has a divisive effect. The issue here which is of paramount importance is the fact that we are all an oppressed people and only by unity can we overcome our oppression. This unity will never be achieved if specific groups fail to resist the carrot offered and start to wander off in different directions. This further divides and fragments us. We are a diversity of peoples with a diversity of cultures and backgrounds. We came originally from different parts of the world, bringing a variety of cultures and languages – but we are now united through a common experience. The common thread running through all our lives here is oppression through discrimination and racism. Each group must retain its own national identity whilst at the same time renewing its commitment to unite, campaign and agitate in the common struggle.

Our diversities remain but our common experience of systematic discrimination should lead us to concentrate all our efforts on achieving unity. Only by unity and solidarity can we withstand such discrimination.

This is what Black groups must strive to achieve – unity and organisation to ensure we win our basic human rights. The divide and rule ploys are constantly being used to keep us apart and widen the gaps between us but these will be ineffective if we make a concerted effort to protect ourselves against such divisive moves.

Black teachers as a group are exploited and oppressed by the British education system with its hierarchical divisions of sex, class and, most predominantly, race. Hierarchy is frowned upon when associated with the Eastern caste system of Hinduism but is made to seem right and justifiable in the British class system. Under this apparently 'natural' and 'superior' system people are alienated and discriminated against. As Black teachers we experience oppression through overt and covert racism which is used to manipulate situations to our disadvantage. Case histories show that Black teachers with greater experience and vastly superior qualifications are bypassed and overlooked when applying for promotion. This is even true when the jobs in question are in areas such as Mother Tongue teaching and Anti-racist work where the contributions of Black teachers have been instrumental in the development of such work.

Asian teachers, for example, who are fluent in three or more languages and conversant with a number of dialects have applied for Scale posts as ESL or EFL teachers and been turned down in favour of a monolingual White, Anglo-Saxon teacher often with little or no teaching experience. These Asian teachers are probably among the legions known to spend hours of their 'home time' translating into various languages – Bengali, Gujarati, Punjabi, Urdu, etc – texts which are then used by White teachers who give no credit to the person whose linguistic skills made the work possible. Schools which are recognised as first class 'bi-lingual' schools, frequently have an Asian teacher devoting hours and hours to the bi-lingual initiatives and receiving no credit for her/his vital support. She/he is taken for granted and seen as a non-entity.

Similarly, Black teachers who take an active part in organising and planning educational policies find that their ideas and strategies are copied wholesale by White teachers who claim the innovatory practices as their own. The credit for the initiative is now given to these 'plagiarisers' who use the success of these practices to their own advantage. Black teachers feel they can no longer afford to sit back and allow others to get away with this kind of plagiarism. We will no longer accept this situation complacently in which others take the praise and land the jobs by usurping our ideas and practices.

Black teachers are fully capable of making their own decisions and participating fully in the decision-making process. We no longer are prepared to accept a situation in which we are forced to carry out policies affecting us directly but which we have not been involved in shaping. For far too long we have been simply the invisible work-force, slogging away and giving our 'liver-string' to no recognisable avail. We have been used as the labour force in general to do all the menial chores and dirty work – in the NHS, transport, the various manual industries and as domestics and cleaning staff. The time has now come for us to become more visible and audible in positive and constructive ways – ways by which we are less known. We have waited for more than half a century for the powers that be – in successive Governments and LEAs – to see us in this positive light and to acknowledge our presence and our value.

Black people in all strata of society and in every field of work have sat back and said 'This is as far as we can get; we cannot get any further here because this is what society has decreed for us'. This sense of resignation and abdication has followed years of trusting people who feel highly threatened by our very presence and who have deliberately enforced policies that left us in limbo. No matter how well qualified or experienced we are, we are destined to remain on the third or fourth rung of the ladder of success (that is if we're on the ladder at all).

The injustice of these discriminatory practices impelled by racist attitudes, must be openly challenged by all of us who are affected by them and by the white radicals on our side. This society demoralises our ego and chucks us into compartments where we are to stay unquestioning. We must challenge this now! For too long we have sat back and allowed ourselves to be carried along in the tide of events without any resistance. It seems as if we have abdicated from the fight for our rights. It is high time that as Black teachers, we begin to do something positive to correct this imbalance.

Black teachers, like Black people in general, have always been at the bottom of the system – Scale 1 for 16 or 17 years; supply teachers; temporary terminal teachers; short term contract teachers – these are all proof of the blatant discriminatory practices which we suffer.

Black teachers, like Black people in general, are often treated as if they were invisible. Black teachers in the promotion queue become especially invisible. Headteachers are renowned for giving scale posts to their own favoured, special person. This favourite beneficiary is not likely to be a Black teacher, however long she/he has been on the staff. There is no set pattern or procedures for appointing staff to posts of responsibility. So much depends on the whims of the heads. The allocation is so haphazard that even teachers who have just finished their probationary year may be appointed. The one virtual certainty is that it won't be a Black teacher who is appointed even if she/he has been teaching in the very school for years.

It would be even more of a miracle if an experienced

The Ladder of Success *Lynette Hubah/Sue Birchall*

Black teacher (Scale 1) were to be successful in applying for a Scale 2 post elsewhere. Often they are not even short-listed even when their qualifications, experience and record are highly impressive.

If a survey were to be conducted about the length of service a Black teacher gives in a school before she/he obtains a scale post, one would be extremely shocked at the number of years served. 8 years would be fairly typical!

Here is one case of an Asian teacher who in desperation asked, 'What will happen to me? Will I ever get a scale post?' This despair has been made more acute because of the probationer who came to her school at the same time. This probationer, at the end of her *first* year, was immediately put on the 'assigned' staff of the school while the Asian teacher remained on Divisional staff after 16 years. The Asian teacher told the head that she would like to be considered for the same assigned post. Of course the request was duly 'considered'! She is still on divisional staff after 20 years!

The educational system is so riddled with biased attitudes and is totally submerged in institutional racism. There have been cases where Black women teachers have played the piano for school assemblies, for concerts and been responsible for all the other musical activities in the school only to find that when a scale post becomes available, it is advertised outside – despite the fact that for many other posts an internal candidate was appointed. The jewel of this anecdote is that the Black teachers concerned were still expected to play the piano for assemblies despite somebody else being appointed and paid extra as the official Music post holder.

Inspectors are known to have chosen teachers with limited experience (sometimes less than 4 years) and set them up in other schools as acting deputy heads – to gain experience! What about all the other teachers who have applied unsuccessfully for these posts, including Black teachers with substantial experience and proven results.

Black teachers have not been given the same opportunities to develop their careers as their colleagues.

The root cause of this inequality seems to be the assessment of competence of Black teachers by heads and inspectors. There is no set pattern or precise criteria for promotion. It is such a subjective, variable decision. There is no conformity or set pattern between school or heads. This lack of any fair and agreed set procedure for all schools to follow has contributed to the virtual absence of Black teachers in any senior posts – a fact that would surely be proved by any independent research.

This is a very revealing and pathetic state of affairs, when the enrolment of some schools, may be 85% to 98.5% Ethnic Minority children and when there are highly qualified, experienced and capable teachers from that minority group either in the same schools or elsewhere. Even if there are such teachers in the same school, they are exploited and effectively manipulated, once their vital services have been drained of their usefulness.

Black teachers are also constantly aware of various kinds of subtle harassment which they encounter in their every-day place of employment, from those in Authority-Post-holders, Senior teachers, Heads and Inspectors. The seemingly well-meaning suggestions, the overbearing petty fault findings, the inconsequential directives and the mind boggling criticism, e.g. arrangement of furniture in the classroom, the type of exercise books the children are using, the grouping of the children, the seating arrangements, the handwriting on the blackboard, the formation of letters, (when there is no fixed handwriting policy in the school) the marking of books, the frequency of listening to children's reading, the record keeping, the way schemes are used, the use of equipment either adequately or not, cupboards to be cleared, of apparatus which is not in constant use, hanging on to odds and ends, bits and pieces (time and energy spent preparing these are not considered or the fact that these time-saving devices/ apparatus may be needed momentarily and therefore essential to be kept on 'tap'), the standard of work is not up to 'mark', the tittle-tattle tales behind one's back; the public reprimands for arriving late for assemblies (no consideration for the classroom activities which may justifiably explain the delay and which are often of greater interest to the children than the heads' assemblies).

One can continue this tirade endlessly but this is the nitty-gritty of the kind of harrassment which Black people face.

At lunch-time staff meetings, when any number of activities might delay the teacher, there is the tendency to make a big issue out of the late arrival. There is a general unwillingness to listen to any justifiable explanations. These petty ways of getting at Black teachers are ostensibly the heads' way of maintaining 'professional' standards but it is often a subtle form of racial harrassment. The kind of petty fault-finding which most Black staff experience is only directed at White staff who become 'troublesome' to the school and are selected by the establishment for the 'chop'.

These constant, if apparently mundane happenings, tend to undermine the confidence of Black teachers. They become anxious to please and to do the right thing according to the Staff Code. As a result they often accept the less favourable teaching arrangements frequently made for them. This may lead to a decline in the overall standard achieved by the teachers concerned. Certainly its demoralising effect makes their job more difficult in all ways.

A brief example at this juncture to illustrate the 'all-benevolent' attitude of most white staff. These attitudes reflect the deep-seated psychological feelings of superiority engendered by racism which lead to less able and less qualified people assuming positions of authority.

In one school an Asian teacher was on half-day release for an in-service course. All her duties were arranged so that she could do them while she was in school. A White teacher was ill but had come to school. The services of the supply teacher were retained for the benefit of this teacher. There was also another 'floater' present. In this school teachers could mutually exchange duties if certain days were inconvenient. This was the acceptable practice, but gradually exchanges were very blatantly made without consulting the teachers concerned! Teachers who objected very strenuously were ignored and of coure the response was nil, as there was little backing from the White staff. Two black teachers found that it was their duties which were changed. They were both on in-service courses and found that they were being given extra duties. The atmosphere was becoming quite fraught and came to a head when the duty of the returned 'ill' teacher (White) was changed and the added duty/load was put on one of the day-release teachers who had her normal playground duty, which she did while she had a very heavy cold. Another Black teacher who is seen as an agitator and who was already in the staff bad books, started a discussion of the added duties. There was a heated argument and the superior, condescending attitude of the White staff belittled the Black teachers for even daring to question the 'exchanged duty', but the black teachers persisted that the extra load was not warranted for this Asian teacher. They also emphasised that there were two extra teachers in the school to support the ill White teacher and it was suggested that one of these two 'support' teachers might be willing to do the duty, seeing that they were all so concerned about the 'ill' teacher!

The argument was going nowhere, and the Asian

teacher decided that she would not do the duty! Tales were taken back to the Head, who stormed, with great panache, into the Staffroom and without listening to the whys and wherefores of the discussions insisted that the Black teacher do the duty. Not only that, the Head insisted that the Black teacher should do the playground duty for the rest of the week! Adding insult to injury! Of course anyone with a tongue in their mouth would retaliate to such an unfair and uncalled for directive from the Head. Another discussion was attempted but this led to further argument with the Black teacher still refusing to do the duty. The Head, with her panache, stormed out of the staffroom instructing the Black teacher that she had to do the duty that day and for the rest of the week. If this was not done, this teacher would be reported to the Inspectors for insubordination!

This is the kind of power structure in which Black teachers work. The insensitive, callous decision, regardless of the strain which was purposely and spitefully inflicted on another human being – a woman like themselves but a Black woman! A Black woman, who in their eyes, was enjoying the *privilege* and *honour* of attending a day release course, but somehow or other she must pay for this prestigious 'handout'. 'It is only through our good graces you are being allowed to attend this course.' The overwhelmingly patronising attitude! This kind of injustice dressed up as fair play is only one example of the many wrongs meted out to Black teachers in the performance of their duty. The power game is a mighty powerful one.

Black teachers are frequently given withdrawal groups for reading, language, maths, etc. These teachers give vital support to the classroom teachers. These supernumerary teachers in the primary sector may be kept 'floating' either voluntarily or otherwise. After years of this kind of positive, constructive contribution, they are flung back into the classroom with difficult children and children who have been consistently underachieving. In this excessively difficult teaching situation they are *now* without any extra support, the vital support which they previously had extended to other teachers. No acknowledgement or recognition of this previous support is taken into consideration. In fact, the Black teachers' efforts are maligned and a multitudinous number of faults are found with them.

One case which came to the attention of one of the Black Teachers' groups was of such a teacher. To crown it all, this Asian woman teacher, when put back into the classroom situation was told by the Head, the very same week, that the Inspectors were coming to inspect her classroom teaching! Marvellous, isn't it? This – after more than seventeen years teaching in this country and four years doing group work. The affrontery of this despicable code of behaviour with which Black teachers are inflicted! I emphasise what I said earlier – the root cause of this problem appears to be the assessment of competence of Black teachers by their colleagues, heads and inspectors.

In contrast, White teachers seem to be assessed by different and more liberal criteria.

It is not customary for White teachers to be given groups to work with when there are Black teachers available. The exceptions are part-timers and those seen as less competent. When White teachers are given responsibility for the group work done in a school, they are almost always treated much more favourably. Their ideas are acclaimed as innovatory and their practices as the solution to the learning difficulties of the 'problem' children – particularly the Black children. The real factors contributing to these difficulties – teacher racism, poor discipline and lack of motivation among others – are never considered.

White teachers doing group work are often rewarded for their effort – how different from the Black experience! Fame is bestowed on these White teachers – their colleagues, the heads and the inspectors are instrumental in the false advancement of their careers. The fact that successful results in small groups of 4 or 5 children does not guarantee similar success with full classes of 25 to 30 is conveniently ignored. These 'successful' teachers very rarely return to class teaching. Instead they are often promoted to advisory teachers.

In view of all this it is little wonder that so many of our children, (Black and White) emerge from 11 years of compulsory schooling, semi-literate and without the tools necessary to make their way in society.

The kind of favoured opportunities described above never land at the feet of Black teachers – regardless of their ability and experience. Regardless too, of how innovative and supportive their work has been. Even their rights as human beings living in a so-called civilised society are denied them. Black teachers are seen simply as the labour force to get on with the job.

In most cases Black teachers who are doing group work are treated as supplies/floaters/supernumaries, whose main task is to fill in for others. Because of their kind of timetable which can be changed at any time and for any reason, they have to be very adaptable and inventive in their work but this evidence of their teaching skill is totally overlooked. This kind of supernumerary teaching has been operating in primary schools for many years and as such, though of low prestige, seemed reasonably secure. Now with all the cuts in education, this one advantage has disappeared. Similarly, secondary teachers are also now in a precarious position because of schools amalgamating. There are many specialist teachers on the staff of these amalgamated schools who have no specific timetables. They are kept as floaters, filling in as supply teachers and are expected to take classes for which they are not as qualified to teach. They become teachers in shortage subjects where there are often more underachievers. They therefore, become 'remedial' teachers of 'difficult' children. For supernumerary staff – about 85% of whom are Black – contracts are not permanent and salaries are note safeguarded. Their position is diabolical and their future uncertain, to say the least.

Recently the NUT have negotiated with ILEA and with other LEAs for permanent contracts for these teachers. Hackney Black Teachers Group are also making representations to ILEA to have the supernumerary status abolished. But in the present climate of government restrictions on spending and enforced cuts in the education service, it is the Black teachers who will be the first to go. In fact the ILEA have already published in *Contact* and in official circulars sent to every school, several proposals aiming to encourage voluntary retirement and redundancies on far from satisfactory terms.

Children constantly see Black teachers in subordinate and nondescript, mundane roles without any position of authority or status. Children are very sensitive to the attitudes of people and we discredit their ability to size up this 'superior' White situation. Years of this kind of servitude is in itself underming the confidence of the Black child and there are rebellious and antagonistic feelings in the young, which display themselves in general attitudes to school, learning and authority. The deficit syndrome which affected Black children, which made them educationally sub-normal (Bernard Coard's book of the 1960's) is still at the root of our Black children ending up as underachievers.

The same kind of deficit syndrome also affects the Black teachers, not because of inadequate qualifications or experience or lack of successful teaching, but the deep-seated psychological feelings resulting from centuries of Imperialistic rule. (The genocide of indigenous people of North America, Slavery, British Rule in India, South Africa and Northern Ireland are all historical happenings which show how one race has dominated and trampled on another. This domination continues today and will do until we organise actively to halt it.)

Many of the Black teachers working here now were trained abroad in the country of their origin. They arrived in the Sixties but are still at the bottom of the hierarchical education system! This country has not yet produced many full-fledged Black British teachers. We have seen White teachers sent on exchange schemes, spending a year in the colonies/islands and then returning as the 'reputable experts'. Overnight it seems, they know all about us, our cultures, our historical background, our life-style of centuries of integration, which has made us a highly adaptive cosmopolitan people. These 'overnight' experts are given top posts, as advisors, dishing out their limited knowledge about us. The White establishment ignores the fact that the root base of the problem lies right here in our midst – not far away in our countries of origin. It lies in the racism in our society and we have been suffering the effects of it for many a year.

Another incident to illustrate the extent of the 'expertise' with which Black teachers are bombarded by these superior White, all-knowledgeable colleagues:

One teacher, who trained and taught abroad for several years before coming to this country in the Sixties is now doing peripatetic work, goint to different schools. The teacher she is replacing has just passed her probationary year. This young White lady sees herself as an expert and would like to dictate to her more experienced colleague about what to do and how to do it, in the classroom. This would be more acceptable if the suggestions were viable, educational ones; *if* these 'suggestions' ensured educational advancement for the children concerned. Many of the children are bi-lingual and the inexperienced teacher knows little about ways of supporting their learning or about the acquisition and development of the relevant skills. She has very low expectations of them. The experienced

Black teacher is of the opinion that children are not being extended sufficiently at this stage of their development. The position is 'in limbo' now but it seems as if it is expected that the experienced teacher should subordinate her professional judgement based on thirtyfive years of experience of successful teaching, to that of the inexperienced White teacher! She is expected to abdicate her rights. The Black teacher is keenly aware of the educational needs of these children and of the high standards her classes have always achieved, particularly in the three R's – a most outdated concept in today's climate of education but which most parents expect from schools.

ABDICATION? PERSEVERANCE? VICTIMISATION? What shall it be? Whose assessment of competence will determine this case? Is it to be another of the so many instances where a Black teacher has to climb down and be viewed as a second-rate teacher, especially when this Black teacher has an established record of successful teaching? The affrontery of it! No credit is given to this Black teacher's years of experience. This is one of those cases when preconceived, stereotyped perceptions lead to viewing teaching methods as too formal, but basically it is because of the White teachers' preconceived ideas that these 'poor' children are so 'deprived' and 'mentally deficient' that the school has now got to provide all the prerequisites of 'readiness for learning' – a syndrome which has affected all Black children educated here in the last 25 years. What then is education? Maybe we need to re-examine the role and purpose of education!

The preconceived and stereotyped views of certain groups are a clear expression of the endemic racism in this society. Teaching against racism in the educational institutions cannot be effectively dealt with as long as Black teachers are systematically discriminated against. The forms of discrimination are so subtle and devious and insidious that Black teachers are loth to believe that what is happening is really so! It is so unbelievable that we have continued to underestimate the extent of racism!

We were more than welcomed when there was a need for Blacks to supplement the labour force of this country, but now that we have settled here, this permanency is not acceptable and divisive means are employed to make us disgruntled and perpetually dissatisfied.

ILEA has set out an ANTI-RACIST Policy for schools. Each school has to produce an Anti-racist policy and code of practice for itself. This is very interesting and highly commendable. ILEA's Initiative and Multi-Ethnic education in schools is a set of five documents which were sent out to schools, to be 'studied' concurrently with other papers – 'guidelines' – but the question is, 'What will be the outcome of all these documents produced by all of ILEA's schools? Is there going to be a collating of all these documents? And once these documents are submitted to the Authority what exactly is going to happen? Who is going to 'check' that certain practices in schools are improving? How is the position of the Black teacher going to be improved? The 'paper chase' is perpetually with us and these are all ways of defusing a highly explosive situation!

These initiatives *Race, Sex and Class* have resulted from several one-day Conferences held by the Authority over a long period. The majority ruling party's awareness of the plight of Black people has perhaps been increased by the tide of events, e.g. the Brixton riots and the Scarman Report, the under-achievement of Black children, etc., and these sociological events/problems have led to the current initiatives by ILEA.

The several 'consultative' one-day conferences spread over several months were well attended by a good cross-section of the Community. Black people from all walks of life attended and in the presence of the white power structure voiced their grievances and put forward proposals for combatting the problems of racial disadvantage. I must mention here that quite a lot of our 'elevated' Blacks, chaired these meetings and were the main speakers on the forum. But these ploys have been used before. There was the endless talking and the churning over of the never-ending deluge which we Black people face. Black people have been on the operating table for far too long, researched with, experimented upon, dissected into small pieces and thrown to the sharks. It is most difficult to get one cohesive Black 'body'. The Black people themselves are being manipulated and exploited by the 'powers that be' and by their own very narrow concept of a problem which encompasses broader issues. They are bought off by the 'carrot' which is offered and kept just beyond their reach!! We are led to the water but 'they' won't let us drink! We must wake up to these ploys and be fully aware of them.

Consultation after consultation for nearly half a century! These consultation meetings are irrelevant and increasingly irritating to those of us who have to face racism every day, and who are the victims of racial discrimination. Numerous studies and reports have clearly identified what central government, local authorities, employers and other agents and institutions should do. There is no shortage of blueprints. 'Units' have been set up – job enticements for the 'boys and the girls' – Ethnic Minority, Equal Opportunity, Education Liaison Officers, Divisional Co-ordinators, Multi-ethnic Co-ordinators, Community Liaison Officers, Anti-racists Officers, etc. and a host of other sub-groups/subcommittee to look into the problems of the Black Community – parents, children and teachers 'en masse' These are well orchestrated devices, tongue-in-cheek ploys, toothless bulldogs to subvert the threat to a system which has been operating quite successfully for centuries of British imperialistic rule.

The quantifiable facts have been closely documented for more than two and a half decades, there is no shortage of the evidence, what is lacking is the sustained and determined positive action to see this problem through.

We the black community, the black teachers and the black children, are highly disillusioned by all these well-intentioned units. We have to awaken to the fact that our so-called Black 'intellegentia' and some of the White liberals, do-gooders/benefactors are inadvertently perpetuating false impressions and we the Black community, the Black teachers and the Black children end up being the victims of a mass deception by the divergent means employed to subvert and defuse the problem.

The Equal Opportunities Unit headed by a Black woman, has one person dealing with 'Teaching Staff'. This one person has to deal with thirty thousand (30,000) teachers. This is an impossible workload for anyone to deal with. This applies equally to all the people employed in the newly created posts – co-ordinators, liaison officers, etc. All the good intentions of these working committees seem quite feasible but they are all understaffed and submerged in bureaucracy. They often collect the same information and duplicate each other's efforts. So how can the committees get started and begin to make any headway?

Equal Opportunities – but equal opportunities for whom? That is the salient question. Is the appointment of a Black woman as the head of the Unit, another form of tokenism? Because of the bureaucracy of the establishment will this person be able to make any ripples in a system which has been operating for so long and which is so deeply entrenched? Some blacks may now see these 'elevated' persons as the magicians who will wave their wand and miraculously get rid of the hideous and insidious cancer which has affected us and replace it by a harmonious world of equal rights and opportunities. The white establishment are now also looking very critically at this 'elevated' person as are other well-positioned black people. The Establishment is also expecting wonders from this 'Wonder Woman' casting her golden lariat to bring about the miraculous release! She must be accountable to them too. Credit must be given to them for being the equal opportunity, anti-racist, anti-sexist employer. But will she be able to be a 'free' agent to exercise her duties as she sees fit, without restrictions? These ventures are still on the launching bases and one can give an educated guess at how long it will take before a successful 'launch' is on its way!

We as Black teachers have to educate the majority of the White to what their racism is, and how it has affected us through the years. We Black teachers have to run the racism awareness courses for the majority Whites. We have suffered the effects of racism, we are the oppressed ones, we know what it has done to us, to our children, to our very lives. We are the ones to tell our White colleagues the kinds of insidious discrimination we have suffered at their hands by their callous insensitivity! This does of course exclude the 'free' White anti-racists who are standing side by side with their Black colleagues to bring about the elimination of discrimination on grounds of race and sex in education and the wider society.

There are certain White liberal groups, such as ALTARF, who have been aware of the plight of Black teachers and through concerted effort, have committed themselves to the fight against racism and fascism in all its manifestations. ALTARF's members are actively trying to combat racism and through this commitment they are gaining recognition from Black colleagues. Black teachers must recognise and acknowledge ALTARF and other groups who stand with them int his fight.

The Teachers' Unions have always taken a low profile with racial issues and when Black teachers have been blatantly discriminated against by Heads (often executives in the Unions or close friends of these executives), colleagues and the authority, the Unions have maintained their position of 'lying low' and 99.9% of the time Black teachers get no positive constructive help from the Unions. Black teachers' cases have always been considered 'not strong enough' to warrant the Union's intervention . "You are doing this in temper!" "This is frivolous." "We can't handle your case." "You have not got any proof." (How can one prove a racist incident?) This is the kind of response Black teachers have received when through despair they seek aid from their Unions. Consider too, that most people, especially Black, join the Teachers' Unions to protect themselves against any misfortunes. What then is the protection?

But, glad to say the Hackney NUT has now begun to take up cases for Black teachers and they have shown an awareness of the problems of Black and Ethnic Minority teachers. This awareness – particularly of the growing abuse of Black teachers contracts – led Hackney NUT to campaign for a change in the position of Black teachers within the ILEA. This interest led to a day's conference in March 1983 when Black teachers turned up in great numbers from Hackney – Division 4. As a result another Conference wholly organised by Black teachers from the Hackney Group was held. This one day conference was a landmark in the annals of the Black teachers in the ILEA. This was the first London-wide conference sponsored by ILTA during school time and we the Black teachers had cover for this day's conference from our White NUT colleagues. The Hackney Black teachers' group have since organised another conference at which the Inner London Black Teachers' Group was formed. The delegates from the ten divisions will organise further meetings and activities to extend the work throughout ILEA. This is all part of the process of getting more Black teachers to become more active in the fight for our equality and recognition of our worth to the system and the Society. The need to express our deep dissatisfaction re our position as Black teachers within the ILEA was the driving force, and we felt that our present position in schools would be further undermined if we did not act now.

Black teachers have a formidable task ahead. We need to be dedicated and determined in our struggle to achieve equal rights and status. We need to be unified and organised if we are to succeed.

1984 ILEA HEADTEACHER APPOINTMENTS
(GLC Anti-Racist Year ILEA Anti-Racist Initiatives?)
From an idea by Hackney Black Teachers' Group

Philip Wolmuth

IMMIGRATION NATIONALITY & UNCERTAINTY

John Wright

(from Tutors Notes . Social Education Quintin Kynaston School 1981)

INTRODUCTION

Quintin Kynaston has gone further than most London schools in thinking through and discussing the implications for school policy of serving a multiracial and multicultural community. As a comprehensive school, Q.K. regards the educational needs of all students as being of equal importance. The school has a clear policy for dealing with racist activity, and Quintin Kynaston's Multi-Ethnic Working Party is engaged in a long term review of curriculum and policy towards the English language and mother-tongue needs of bilingual students.

As a community school, Q.K. will be increasingly involved in attempting to define and meet the broader educational needs of students and their families. The Social Education unit on immigration and nationality will, hopefully, contribute to this process. In addition, the unit will help make clear to students and the local community the extent to which Quintin Kynaston staff both recognise and welcome the now permanent multi-racial nature of British society.

The following is intended for use as background reading or as a discussion document by members of Q.K. staff. None of it is intended to be used directly as teaching material.

AIMS & CONTENT OF THE SOCIAL EDUCATION UNIT ON IMMIGRATION & NATIONALITY

Anyone concerned with school students now needs to know something about immigration law: partly in order to be able to advise students and their families in a crisis; more importantly, to be able to help them avoid problems in the first place. Unfortunately it is not always possible to forsee and avoid problems. . .

In July 1980 in Nelson, Lancashire, two schoolgirls aged 9 and 12 were taken from their classes by policemen. They were placed in a children's home in another town some miles away and a government minister decided that they should be sent to Pakistan – despite the fact that there was no-one there to look after them; that they had been in Britain for five years and that neither of them spoke a word of Urdu. The case was publicised in the local press but received no coverage nationally. Similar cases have occurred in other parts of the country and have usually received publicity only at a local level. In Oxford, in 1979, a girl of 7 and a boy of 8 were threatened with removal. A local campaign eventually saved them. Parents, teachers, heads of Oxford colleges and a member of the House of Lords were among the hundreds of local people involved. But not all families are this lucky. Some are deported without schools or local press hearing anything about it.

Aims

The aims of the Social Education unit on immigration and nationality are: First – to let all students know that staff at Q.K. expect to be told of problems which they and their families are facing. Second – to provide information, advice and support, both through the staff in the school and by arranging for people who can help to come into school to talk to students and their families.

Content

The unit will consist of:

1. A series of year assemblies on the theme of 'Q.K. as an international community'.
2. Follow-up discussions in tutor groups and some or all of the following:
   a. Conducting class surveys to find out where we all come from, whether from another part of the world or another part of Britain. Results to be charted or mapped.
   b. Personal writing describing students' own experiences of 'leaving and arriving', using students' writing as a stimulus.
   c. Writing a poem expressing the sense of change or loss which people who have moved home usually experience, using students' writing as stimulus.
   d. As an extended project, students agreeing to interview grandparents about their experiences of moving home. Interviews could be conducted in students' first languages and translated into English in school.
3. Leaflets and/or letters to parents will be available for tutors to hand out to students who want them, containing details of the dates and times of the advice surgeries being arranged with West Hampstead Law Centre.
4. The advice surgeries. Two lawyers from the Law Centre will come to school for two afternoon/early evening sessions. They will discuss problems with any students and families who attend.

SUGGESTIONS FOR HANDLING CLASS DISCUSSION ON IMMIGRATION

Problems

Raising the issue of immigration in the classroom will inevitably prompt discussion and argument. It is important that the teacher has accurate information to hand, should it be needed. Equally, it is important to be aware of the assumptions which underlie many of the arguments about immigration to Britain. For example, it is a common misconception that there are more black people in Britain than is the case. Yet if a teacher corrects this misconception with a simple factual statement ("There are not twenty million black people living in Britain. The figure is nearer to 3½ million") she risks implying that black people are only all right so long as there are not many of them. Which begs the question: how many are acceptable? 5 million? 10 million? The danger when arguing about numbers is that people are dehumanised, treated as statistics, even if the original intention is well-meaning.

There is another danger, equally obvious: that of setting-up in the classroom a discussion situation in which the teacher (having prepared for the lesson) has all of the facts at here fingertips and is pushed repeatedly into the position of having to say, "No, that's not true. The real reason/story/figure. . ."

Possible solutions

How can we manage class discussion without slipping into the kind of debate which accepts the racist assumption that numbers are what matter (consequently affirming prejudice and insulting black students present in the class) and without posing as authoritarian and sole providers of the truth? Three possible solutions are explored in this section: First, rather than directly contradicting what students say, encourage them to question their own sources of information. Second, rather than directly contradicting what students say, encourage them to ask why it is that immigration becomes a controversial issue at particular times (Why now, when immigration has all but ceased? What *use* do politicians make of the issue of immigration?) Third, when misconceptions have to be countered by the teacher's providing students with accurate information, it may be useful to do this in a way which will encourage them to think through to examining and discussing the *real* anxieties which may underlie their concerns about race.

Questioning sources of information

The national media (press and T.V.) provide most of information. Do students implicitly trust newspapers and T.V. on other issues? If not, why shouldn't they question them as sources of information on immigration? This example may go back a bit too far in time for our students, but most teachers will remember how the press treatment of the arrival of Asian families from Malawi, in 1976, sparked off racist campaigns.

Malawi Asians, as British passport-holders, had every right to apply to come to Britain. Due to circumstances in Malawi, a small number of families arrived in Britain. The *Daily Mirror* headlined: NEW FLOODS OF ASIANS. The *Daily Express* headlined: ASIAN FLOOD WARNING AS MORE FLY IN. The *Sun* had: M.P.'s RAGE OVER THREAT OF NEW ASIAN INVADERS. The *Sun* reported that there were 20,000 British passport holders in Malawi. The *Daily Mail* put the figure at 40,000. The official government estimate was 6,800 (House of Lords written reply 27.5.76). The British High Commission in Malawi thought this number was too high. Estimates by informed members of the Asian community in Malawi varied, but none exceeded 6,000.

As for the question of how many of these people, legally entitled to enter Britain, actually came here: sixty passport holding heads of families came in May of 1976 and a further 45 in June of that year. (*Report from Malawi – The Past, Present and Future of British Asians.* Pub. Joint Council for the Welfare of Immigrants. 1976.)

More recently, as a follow-up to Mrs Thatcher's

comments on British culture being 'rather swamped', the *Daily Mail* printed this story:

> ONE IN FIVE BABIES ARE COLOURED
> What is the background to the issues raised by Tory leader Mrs Thatcher? There is good reason to believe that a fifth of all children being born in Britain are coloured . . . (1.2.78)

This was 200% wrong. The statistic they based the article on was of births to mothers who had come to Britain and included families from Malta, Gibralta and Cyprus. And the cultural proportion was 1 in 14 births. A few days later the *Daily Mail* admitted having published 'an inaccurate report on a delicate issue'. They printed an apology at the foot of a column on an inside page.

What use do politicians make of the issue of immigration?

Students will be able to discuss this question on the basis of their own experience of the media, and by comparing the words of different politicians. Some of the following extracts, however, may be useful as historical background. . .

Anti-semitic speeches made in the late 19th century contain phrases and sentiments which sound familiar today:

> *"It would be a serious matter if the type of population which is now to be found in many districts in the East End, where there is a strong alien element, were to become at all a common type in the poorer districts in our large cities. It would mean, my Lords, that these classes would become to a greater extent non-English in character, and that, both in physique and in moral and social customs, they have fallen below our present by no means elevated standard"* (Lord Hardwicke 1898)

"Not a day passes but English families are ruthlessly turned out to make room for foreign invaders. Out they go to make room for Rumanians, Russians and Poles. Rents are raised fifty to a hundred per-cent, and a house which formerly contained a couple of families living in comparative decency is made to contain four or five families living in conditions which baffle description . . . It is only a matter of time before the population becomes entirely foreign . . . The rates are burdened with the education of thousands of children of foreign parents . . . Among the thousands who came here there is a considerable proportion of bad characters, and the competition with home industries extends to burglary and other cognate crimes. I should have thought we had enough criminals of our own. . ."

(Major Evans Gordon 1902)

Evans Gordon supported his speech with extra-parliamentary work which sounds as familiar as his arguments. He formed a militant anti-semitic organisation called "British Brothers' League" and a week before he made the above speech, led 6,000 supporters on a march through Tower Hamlets, shouting abuse at Jews and other 'foreigners'.

A more recent development in British politics is the way in which, once racist sentiments have been aroused, the main parties will compete with each other in trying to satisfy them. The classic example was the General Election campaign in Smethwick in 1964. From the outset the Tory candidate, Peter Griffiths, campaigned on an anti-immigrant line. He was vociferously supported by extreme racist groups. The Labour candidate, Patrick Gordon Walker, tried at first to ignore the issue of immigration. He failed to discuss or challenge the racist assumptions underlying Griffiths call for an end to all immigration. Then, just before the poll, Gordon-Walker made a desperate attempt to win the racist vote from

Griffiths by arguing that it was the Conservatives who were most to blame for immigration:

> *"The whole wave of immigration has occurred since 1961 whilst the Conservatives have been in power. It is false and unfair to blame the Labour Party for immigration"* (Gordon Walker March 1964)

A last minute leaflet, issued just before the poll, urged:

> *"Be fair.*
> *Immigrants only arrived in Smethwick in large numbers during the last ten years —while the Tory Government was in power.*
> *You can't blame Labour or Gordon Walker for that.*
> *Labour favours continued control of immigration, stricter health checks and deportation of those convicted of criminal offence . . ."*

More recently, in the run-up to the last general election, immigration again seemed to be used as a vote catching issue. In October 1976, when their lead over the Labour Party was almost 20 points, the Conservative Party issued a mid-term report on its aims and policies. It was called *The Right Approach,* and immigration took up only one of its seventy pages. By early January 1977, the position had been reversed and Labour led the Conservatives. Mrs Thatcher made her 'swamping' speech on television in late January and (according to a *Daily Mail* opinion poll) the Conservatives swung immediately back into a lead over Labour. The Labour Prime Minister denounced Mrs Thatcher and accused her of using racism to catch votes. But he added that the Conservatives would not be able to do anything to stop immigration which the Labour Government was not already doing. In other words, Labour claimed to be meeting the racists' demands just as firmly as the Conservative Party promised they would if they achieved power.

Subsequent to the formation of a Conservative Government, we have had the Nationality Bill, shortly to become law. While the Labour Party's spokesman on Home Affairs, Roy Hattersley, pledges that the Nationality Act will be repealed immediately the next Labour Government comes to power, it is necessary to remember that no-one is, as yet, sure who will be responsible for drawing-up the next manifesto. In a sense, the pledge is premature. And it is also necessary to remember that the British Council of Churches opposition to the present Nationality Bill is based on the omission of certain principles (nine in all) which they feel any new nationality legislation should embody. Unfortunately these nine principles were also missing from the Green Paper which the last Labour Government produced on nationality, and which could have formed the basis of legislation which a Labour Government may have been enacting at this time, had the Labour Party been successful in the last election.

Corrections, misconceptions and challenging assumptions

Many of the misconceptions surrounding immigration give rise to questions which, on the surface, seem quite reasonable. It is largely the fault of the media that such misconceptions exist, but that does not mean that the questions themselves can be ignored. On the following pages, a number of questions and answers are set out as examples. But statistical answers, in themselves, will rarely be sufficient.

It's just a small island . . . How many more people do you think it can take?

Ever since 1964 more people have been leaving Britain than have been arriving here to settle. In 1972, for example, 190,000 people arrived to settle and 238,000 people left to live elsewhere.
SOURCE: Office for Population Census and Survey's

evidence to the Select Committee on Race and Immigration. HMSO 1973.
Many other European countries have a denser population than we have, e.g. Germany, Belgium, Sweden.
SOURCE: Pan World Atlas.

But we are losing all of our skilled people and getting unskilled people in their place.

In fact, work permits are limited to a professional, skilled and special category of occupations (e.g. hospital and seasonal work). Permits are not issued to unskilled workers.
SOURCE: Civil Liberties: NCCL Guide, Chapter 12. '78.

People coming and going in the professional and managerial group just about balanced each other up in the 11 years between 1964 and 1975. Between 1964 and 1975 about 35% of those entering and 40% of those leaving the country were in the professional/managerial class.
SOURCE: Population Trends 8. 1977.

There is no control at all over the numbers of people coming into Britain.

Immigration of foreign nationals into this country has been restricted since the Aliens Act of 1904. Immigration of Commonwealth citizens has been restricted since 1962. Since the 1971 Act things have been very restricted. There are three categories of people who can come and settle in Britain:
1. Commonwealth citizens whose parents or grandparents were born here;
2. Husbands, wives and other dependents of those already settled here;
3. A limited number of U.K. passport holders who have no other citizenship and no other country to live in.

SOURCE: 1971 Immigration Act.

The main problem at present is that these restrictions are being enforced too rigorously. Many wives and children who have the legal right to joint their husbands in this country are made to wait up to two years before being allowed to enter. These are people who will eventually come to this country, so causing delay serves little purpose.

Being members of the EEC has somewhat confused the issue of immigration restrictions. All EEC nationals have the right to seek employment in other member countries. There are about two hundred million people in the community.

But what about all of those illegal immigrants?

There are special units within the Immigration Service and the police set up to deal with illegal immigration and with people who overstay their visas. They work in close co-operation with similar units in other countries. Yet, given all this, only 809 people were detained in the whole of 1977, of whom 61 were found not to be here legally.

But surely there is a limit to the number of people Britain can take who have a different culture?

There is no such thing as a single 'British' culture. Life-styles and ideas differ according to class, religion, age, geographical area, etc. The British people have originated from several sources: Germany, Norway, Denmark, etc. The idea of a single British culture is erroneous.

People who have come from other parts of the world have simply added an extra ingredient or two to the mix.

Of course, most of the black and Asian people in schools have been born in this country. They are growing up with and helping to create cultures which are as indigenous to this country as any other.

But isn't the black population increasing more rapidly than the white population?

It happens that a larger proportion of the black population is between the ages of 18 to 40 – the age group that has children.

But, in any case, what does it matter?

The racist assumptions underlying many of these questions are quite obvious: white people going out . . . black people coming in; black families having more children . . . etc. The assumptions, as well as the misconceptions on issues of fact, need to be challenged.

Exploring the real anxieties which underlie concerns about race

Yet there are many people who are not particularly prejudiced but who nevertheless feel 'they edge me and mine out of what we are due to'. And 'me and mine', here, has more to do with feelings of loyalty being owed first and foremost to immediate family, than with any racist sentiment. At a time when the economy seems to be locked into a decline; when the social services are being cut and housing shortages are becoming more and more acute; at a time when unemployment has exceeded the 1930's peak . . . it would be surprising if some of the resultant discontent did *not* get directed towards minorities. So, in addition to correcting misinformation and challenging racist assumptions, it is important to accept the seriousness of the economic circumstances facing some of our students. And it is important to stress that, rather than being the *cause* of such circumstances, members of minority ethnic groups are the chief *victims.*

Immigrants sponge off the welfare state . . . it's what they came for.

In 1976 (i.e. before the current and dramatic rise in

unemployment) 91% of all adult males of minority group origin in this country were either working or registered as willing and able to work. This was compared with 77% of the total adult male population. Of course, minority group workers pay taxes and insurance contributions like everyone else.
SOURCE: The Facts of Racial Disadvantage. P.E.P. '76.

They take our jobs

During the 1950's and 1960's there were labour shortages in this country. We welcomed workers from the Commonwealth, just as we had welcomed soldiers from the Commonwealth during the war. Workers wanted to come to Britain because it could offer them a higher standard of living for themselves and their families. Like other countries in Europe, we depended on immigrant workers to pull us out of the debt we were left in after the war. Now, at a time when jobs are scarce, black workers suffer from unemployment to a much greater extent than do white workers.
SOURCE: The Facts of Racial Disadvantage. P.E.P. '76.

They are a drain on the social services

Because the black population is relatively young, they contribute *more* to the social services, and take out less than the rest of the population.
SOURCE: The Economic Impact of Immigration.
C.U.P. 1970.

They get favoured in council housing

The opposite is the case. In fact there are only 4% of Asians and 26% of West Indian families in council housing, compared with 30% of the population as a whole.

A point for discussion
The following section contains a brief outline of immigration legislation in Britain and some notes on the effects of the forthcoming Nationality Act. While this Act is the immediate pretext for tackling immigration as an issue in Social Education, teachers may like to discuss the extent to which this is the ideal forum for the discussion of this matter. Many misconceptions arise from gaps in students' knowledge, for example of:

- Britain's past relationship with the countries of the Commonwealth;
- the economic relationship existing between the UK and the developing countries today;
- traditional causes of population movement;
- the causes and effects of racist thinking and racial discrimination.

To what extent should information of this kind be available to students through the mainstream curriculum (Humanities, Social Studies, History, Geography departments)? Group discussion of a current affairs issue such as the new nationality legislation would be enhanced if students had had the opportunity to acquire the necessary background knowledge. And the problems caused by the teacher's being the sole source of correct information would be minimised.

BRITAIN'S NATIONALITY LAW

Britain's relationship with the rest of the world has altered substantially during the past thirty years. In earlier days Britain was the centre and head of a large Empire, and after the formation of the British Commonwealth retained close ties, especially economic and commercial, with these countries. Our present citizenship of the United Kingdom and Colonies was established by the British Nationality Act 1948, under which any person born in a Colony of the Empire was automatically a citizen of the U.K. and Colonies, and, as late as 1962, these and all other British subjects from anywhere in the Commonwealth could come to Britain without restriction. Once here they had the right to vote, to hold public office and to take jobs in the public sector.

1962

In 1962, the first of many restrictions was placed on the right of citizens of the U.K. and Colonies to enter Britain: The Commonwealth Immigrants Act. The Conservative Home Secretary at the time complained of "a quarter of the globe being able to come in". But as Hugh Gaitskell, Leader of the Opposition pointed out, ". . . that situation existed in 1900, 1910, 1920, 1930 and 1940 . . . in all those years . . . although they could have come, they did not. The simple reason was there were no jobs for them to come to."

The reason for immigration into Britain in the fifties and early sixties was simply that there were jobs to be done. British industry actively recruited overseas for workers to come and do them. The workers who came were legally entitled to come, as citizens of the United Kingdom and Colonies.

1968

In 1968, a new Immigration Act was introduced. Its aim was to keep out East African Asians who were being expelled from Kenya. These were legally entitled to enter Britain. They held citizenship of the U.K. and of no other country, and so were not entitled to go anywhere else. In 1973, the European Commission on Human Rights was to conclude that "the Commonwealth Immigrants Act of 1968, by subjecting to immigration control citizens of the United Kingdom and Colonies in East Africa who were of Asian origin, discriminated against this group of people on grounds of their colour or race."

1971

By 1971, the post war boom in the economy had passed. Immigration legislation did not keep out everyone, however. Just black citizens. The 1971 Immigration Act distinguished between citizens of the United Kingdom and Colonies who had a parent or grandparent born in the U.K. and those who did not. This novel mechanism – the patriality clause – closed the door to citizens of the U.K. and Colonies who happened to be black or brown.

It is the conflict between this state of affairs and the letter and spirit of the 1948 Nationality Act (see above) which has lead to the situation where politicians are anxious to establish a new definition of British nationality.

The new legislation

What the government intends is to take the categories of citizens from the immigration law as it now stands and move them sideways into nationality law. Patrial (i.e. white) citizens of the U.K. and Colonies are to become 'British Citizens' with a right of entry to the U.K. and Colonies citizens (i.e. black and Asian citizens) will become either Citizens of the British Dependent Territories or British Overseas Citizens – neither category having an automatic right to enter Britain.

No other rights are defined for any of the three groups, except the right to apply for (which is different to the right to *get*) a passport from the British Government or a Colonial Government. The point of having a passport is to assist one's international movement. Yet the third category, British Overseas Citizen, would actually find its international movement hampered by passports as these would show them as not being admissible to any territory anywhere for which Britain was responsible. So they could not be returned anywhere. This citizenship will not be transferable to wives or children, and as a result some children will be born stateless, in the future, to British Overseas Citizens abroad.

Thus, the Nationality Act will incorporate the racist character of immigration legislation since 1971.

Objections in principle

The British Council of Churches (in addition to numerous political and ethnic minority groups) argues that the creation of a new definition of British citizenship presents the opportunity to redefine citizenship on a non-racist basis. The argument runs as follows: Britain is now irrevocably a multi-racial society. Our national identity is multi-racial. A new Nationality Act should explicitly recognise and welcome this fact. It should avoid, at all costs, making distinctions between people on the basis of skin colour.

Practical consequences

In addition to this objection in principle to what is being proposed, the new Act will have a number of practical effects on ethnic minority communities:

1. The uncertainties in the Act will create further insecurities for ethnic minorities settled in Britain.

2. Commonwealth Citizens resident in Britain since 1973 will lose (in five years time) their automatic right to British Citizenship applications will be subject to the discretion of the Home Secretary. This will affect both West Indians and Asians, and some West Indians may not be aware that they may have become citizens of a Commonwealth country (rather than U.K. citizens) after the independence of their country of birth.

3. Children under the age of 18, who were born in a Commonwealth country and entered Britain before 1973 will lose the automatic right to British citizenship immediately after the Bill becomes law.

Not only will their application for British Citizenship be subject to the Home Secretary's discretion, the different method of application will cost £150 rather than £50. Those affected will notably include some children of West Indian parents, as well as other ethnic minorities.

4. There is no right of appeal against the Home Secretary's refusal of a British citizenship, although more people will be included in his area of discretion.

5. A birth certificate will no longer be proof of U.K. citizenship. All British born children, particularly those with ethnic minority parents, will have to refer to the immigration status or citizenship of their parents before citizenship is established.

6. A few East African Asians resident in Britain with U.K. passports will become British Overseas Citizens, which is considered by many to be of second class status. They will have to apply again for British Citizenship (at a cost of £50).

N.B. ALTARF recommends that school children and parents needing advice are referred to the local law centre. Up to date information on the effects of immigration and nationality legislation is available from: Joint Council for the Welfare of Immigrants, 115 Old Street, London EC1V 9JR. Tel. 01-251 8706.

POLICE IN SCHOOLS

E. Kolenzo, a primary school teacher

When considering the relationship between the police and schools it is necessary to be aware of the role of schools in promoting social control and in instilling values which can be racist, sexist and classist, which is discussed elsewhere in this book. Staff in schools, children and parents are subjected to influences from the media, and it seems that for the last decade the media have been extremely anxious to promote the idea that Black people are potential criminals. This has been exposed in publications which detail the building up of 'beliefs' about Blacks in Britain.[1]

The uprisings in our cities and the clashes with the forces of 'law and order' did not happen purely by accident. The relationship between police and Black people has been fed by this 'belief', nurtured by post-colonial attitudes, and well absorbed by the police, that Black people do not belong here, do not readily fit into 'British' society and have lifestyles which the 'British' outlaw and interpret as criminal.[2] Salman Rushdie has pointed out that the 'British' have imported their past empire into this country and expect to continue to treat the 'subject races' in the same way.[3] Politicians have used this 'alien' approach to feed on the fears of a white working class population feeling the effects of economic decline (in particular Margaret Thatcher's famous 'swamping' speech). It is significant that the present government did not feel the need to fight the 1983 general election on this issue – the job had already been done. The Nationality Act established that if you are Black you will have a hard time proving that you are British . . . Although the Conservative Party boasted in their election campaign that they had abolished the 'sus' laws, they have, in effect, still continued to allow the same abuses of the rights of Black people in the streets. The Police Bill, halted temporarily by the last general election, has been re-introduced and promises, in true 1984 spirit, to be formidable in the powers it gives for arrest, detention and information gathering.[4]

The Bill contains powers to:

1. detain people without charge for up to 4 days with no automatic right to see a solicitor for 36 hours;
2. conduct intimate body searches (of the mouth, anus and vagina) on people who are detained;
3. search people's homes even when they are not suspected of any offence;
4. stop and search people on the streets using 'reasonable force if necessary';
5. set up road blocks around certain areas for 7 days, renewable indefinitely;
6. arrest people on certain grounds even for minor offences such as littering or parking on a yellow line;
7. carry out by force, finger printing, intimate body searches and taking of non-intimate body samples from children as young as 10 years old.

In short, the previously illegal abuse of powers that the police have used against Black people, Irish, Gays and more recently, and with disturbing force, against women and trade unionists, will, if the bill is made law, be perfectly legal and enforced throughout the population. Children are particularly at risk as section 7 shows.

Policing over the past two decades has undergone subtle changes and certain ideas have been promoted as 'new' approaches. Since the Scarman Report, the idea of 'community policing' has been promoted – although it is easy to misunderstand that seemingly comfortable

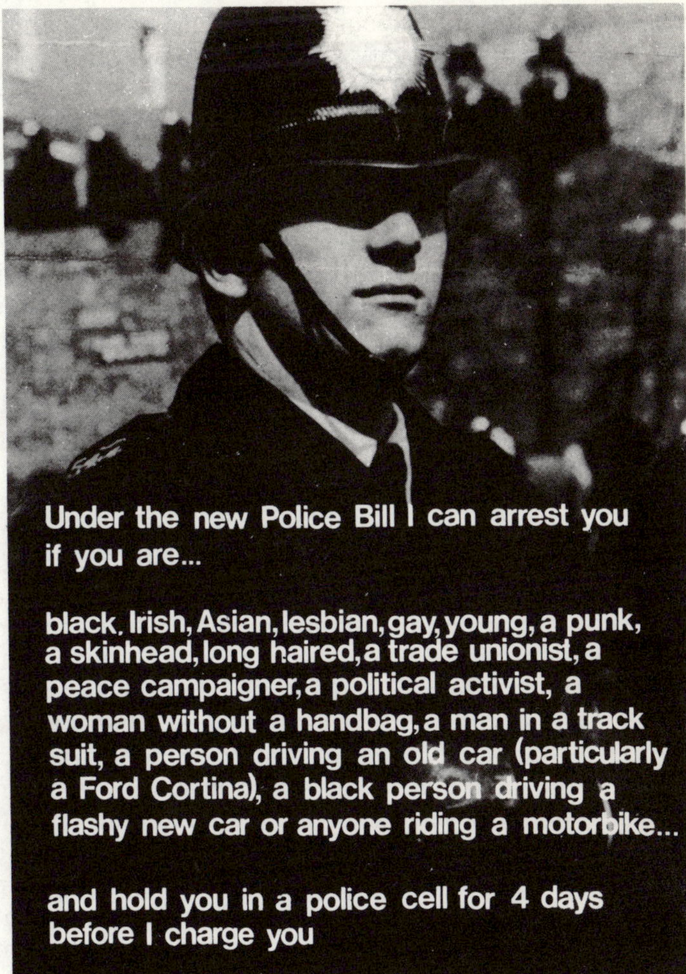

1984 GLC Anti-Racist Year *Photomontage by Cath Tate*

title. One would assume it would mean less technology, machinery and special groups and a move back to the so-called 'friendly bobby' (a myth which has probably only appeared true in country areas in the past where the 'community' was more defined and able to absorb the police officer into its midst – the working class populations of the cities have always been seen as potential law breakers). This conveniently ignores the fact that the police have been training for many years now in counter insurgency and are well able to use sophisticated technology for surveillance. Commander Newman of Scotland Yard was well known in Northern Ireland for promoting 'community policing' alongside hard-line tactics and computerized information gathering. Weapons are now being used quite openly and we, the public, have grown accustomed to hearing that armed police have shot their suspects. This calculated use of weapons and counter insurgency aids (plastic bullets, CS gas, riot shields etc.) has gone hand in hand with the promotion of the beat police officer as a friendly person who cares about his/her beat and therefore wants to get to know everyone. We have to see this in the context of information gathering which is then fed to the police station collator, and as only one aspect of an increasingly complex and wide-ranging state mechanism.[5]

In the recent industrial disputes – that of the National Graphical Association and the Mine Workers strike – the police have been used in vast numbers in a clearly political way to break the strike and uphold management. At Greenham Common it is the same story. Our rights to move around the country are threatened. As trade unionists we are becoming aware of the police state that has been in existence in Northern Ireland for so long.

In the schools we could well be lulled into a sense that welcoming the beat police officer into our school will help the children develop 'a healthy respect for the best side of the police force' and allow the police to 'recognise the values of a multi-cultural society'. These are real opinions expressed by teachers. This rather ignores the real experiences of many of our Primary children, particularly those who are Black (but not exclusively) and certainly can be challenged by Black parents and teachers, and older children. It is significant that the 1983 HMI report 'Police Liaison with the Education Service'[6] assumes that liaison can only be beneficial and warns against those teachers who may seek to discredit it, but nowhere acknowledges the relationship between Black people and the police. This relationship was exposed recently when the Policy Studies Institute report was published and admitted that the Metropolitan Police were normally racist and sexist in their attitudes and behaviour and frequently flouted rules during arrests and questioning.[7]

Are we, then, as teachers, to be seen as colluding with a force which is largely used to control, in a repressive but selective way, street life in our cities? The media continues to delight in the 'Blacks as criminals' image. The first item on the BBC TV news of 21st August 1983, told the story of a child and baby who were threatened by four Black youths in Brixton for money. The parent of the child and baby, who was white, was interviewed, referring to the youths as 'animals'. The police officer in charge was then interviewed to give weight to the story. Obviously an appalling incident, yet, there have been countless cases where Asian men, women, babies and children have been viciously and repeatedly attacked by racist whites.[8] Yet these have never been given the status of first item on the national news. This may well be because most racist attacks against Black people are not even reported because the police have previously failed to take them seriously, and in many cases sympathise with the attackers rather than the victims. But it must also be recognised that, for the media, the main factor is that they are just not as newsworthy. We teachers must understand this process and be aware that for many of the families we are involved with, the police are not to be trusted. The recent case of the Newham 8, where plain clothes police set upon Asian youths, attacked and racially abused them, is an important example. Can we possibly have the right to welcome police officers into schools to gather information on the children?

Naturally, there may be individual police officers who are 'nice people' but they must be seen in the context of the whole operation. John Fernandes, previously a lecturer in multi-cultural studies at Hendon Police College, in publishing racist essays written by cadets and being dismissed for doing so, helped to expose the fact that the police are not prepared to seriously try to put their house in order, and at the same time indicated the limited value of multi-cultural education. Yet the police frequently publicise their desire to visit every school and there they may be seen attending assemblies, arranging outings, demonstrating dog-handling, running disco-dances, football matches, quizzes, debates as well as warning of dangers on roads and of attacks by strangers. (One wonders how they have time to actually catch real criminals!) Ostensibly this is what they are doing in schools but one officer was overheard telling a headteacher that the police were not really very interested in the finals of the disco-dancing competition but that the real purpose was to get into the school to observe and get to know the children. This is part of what is now known in the Metropolitan area as the 'multi-agency approach'. Information gathered in this way helps to build up a picture of particular families in the area and can then be fed into the station computer. ALTARF as well as other groups have a wealth of evidence to show the extent and the sometimes sinister nature of police involvement in the London area.[9] Police are frequently represented in case conferences and are often consulted informally by pastoral staff about 'disruptive' children.

In East London an Infant Head invited to a police party by the beat policeman was appalled when racist jokes and insults were the order of the day. Another Infant Head in Brixton tried to stop the police continually visiting the school and was blatantly ignored and subsequently found officers having tea with ancilliary staff. There are secondary schools where 'stroppy' or 'anti-police' children were noted by visiting officers conducting debates on the 'riots' and later this was used in evidence against them when they happened to come up before the law. Heads and senior staff in several London schools frequently and regularly call in the police to discipline students who fight or to investigate theft. On many occasions this has been done without prior parental consent. A primary head teacher recently admitted in the T.E.S. that he had handed pupil records over to the police and the Chairman of Croydon Education Authority has sent letters to all schools in the Borough urging head teachers to help the police by monitoring rumours of racial unrest. A parent who questioned the role of the police in her son's school was subjected to investigations into her activities as a teacher and information on her was subsequently passed on to Scotland Yard by the Education Officer! Many teachers and personnel in our education offices see it as their role to pass over information to the police. We, in caring for our children, must be aware of this and be prepared to question and argue in an informed way against the involvement of the police in our schools.

Calls for the 'accountability' of the police force are being made, particularly by Labour Party branches. Some Boroughs have attempted to outflank this demand by setting up their own liaison groups or police committees. These groups are often merely cosmetic and are used to legitimise police action by suggesting 'community support' for what they do. It is debatable whether the 'community', whatever that means, could ever be fully represented and you should check on just

North Paddington Community Darkroom/Philip Wolmuth

how independent groups such as Police Consultative Groups, Police-Community Liaison Groups, and even Police Monitoring Groups are before getting involved with them. Where groups are independent however, they have recorded valuable information on racist incidents and police responses. The work of the Newham Police Monitoring Group is particularly impressive.

The police force is frequently presented as a topic for study within the curriculum of Primary and Secondary schools, even in Nursery schools the police are shown as one of the 'people who help us'. The police 'helped' kill Blair Peach, a teacher, and too often beat up Black youths in cells and many of the children know this. It is essential that children are aware of their rights. By linking with law centres, schools can integrate information on rights, and a study of laws relating to young people into social studies topics. A thorough examination of the history and role of the police within Britain, could be extremely useful, and certainly more valid educationally than filling in the Panda quiz sheets.[10] (This could be studied independently of the usual trite school books on the subject, perhaps using historical evidence and articles in alternative journals, and drawing on experiences of children and parents and other adults, so that the children can compare and make up their minds in an informed way.) Although I would argue against police involvement in any school, I can see the difficulties of isolated teachers in schools where an anti-police line would be interpreted as suspicious in the extreme. Teachers must be careful to align themselves with supporters in and outside school, preferably linking with anti-racist or monitoring groups or progressive law centres, as well as their union branch if it is sympathetic, and should be aware that their opinions will be noted in evidence against them. It is worth pointing out that although ILEA have produced lengthy documents on the case for multi-cultural and anti-racist education,[11] they have never seriously considered this in the light of the authority's policy of encouraging open access to police in its educational institutions.[12] This is an extremely important omission which ALTARF has frequently pointed out in written submissions to ILEA. It has also been discussed in the journal of the Advisory Centre for Education with regard to the rights of children and their parents.[13] The involvement of police in schools is particularly perturbing in the light of police powers regarding immigration checks and enforcement of the Nationality laws. Several schools have been involved in fighting deportations and some parents and children have gone into hiding – nobody wants the police around in such circumstances! It will be impossible for anti-racist initiatives to take root in schools and colleges unless this access is curtailed and the whole conflict brought out into the open.

This must inevitably be only an introduction to the subject. For those wishing to pursue the topic in order to prepare a course of study in school or to enable them to discuss the matter in an informed way with colleagues and parents, I offer the reading list at the end. It is worth noting that several N.U.T. branches have taken decisions recommending members to ban police from schools. Certain schools have also taken this decision quite independently. ALTARF is willing to offer advice and support to anyone wishing to take up this stance and invites evidence of police involvement in schools. This will be treated confidentially. We would also appreciate copies of policies concerning police in schools.

REFERENCES

1 Centre for Contemporary Cultural Studies – *The Empire Strikes Back – Race and Racism in Seventies Britain,* Hutchinson, 1982.
· Hall, Stuart et al – *Policing the Crisis, Mugging, the State, and Law and Order,* Macmillan, 1978.
Race and Class, *Rebellion and Repression* vol. xxiii, Institute of Race Relations.
2. Howe, Darcus – *From Bobby to Babylon,* Race Today, 1980-82.
Macdonald, Ian – *The Creation of the British Police,* Race Today, December '73.
3 Rushdie, Salman – *The New Empire Within Britain,* New Society, 9.12.82.
4 Christian, Louise – *Policing by Coercion, The Police and Criminal Evidence Bill* GLC Police Committee Support Unit, 1983.
Police Committee Support Unit – *Policing London* '82–'84.
5 Bunyan, Tony – *The Political Police in Britain,* Julian Friedman, 1976.
Bunyan, Tony – *The Police Against the People* in Rebellion and Repression.
6 HMI – *Police Liaison with the Education Service,* DES, April, 1983.
7 GLC Police Committee Support Unit – *Policing London* No. 10, December '83.
8 Bethnal Green and Stepney Trades Council – *Blood on the Streets,* 1978.
Newham Monitoring Group – *Newham Monitor*
Race and Class – *Police Against Black People,* 1979.
Wilson, Amrit – *Conspiracies to Assault,* New Statesman, 25.2.83.
9. ALTARF – Newsletters
ALTARF – Conference Report, *Police in Schools,* Sheila Patel 1982.
Riley, Kathryn – *Policing the Police, Teaching the Teachers,* NAME, Multi-racial Education, Spring '82.
Rollo, Joanna – *Police Go Back to School,* Socialist Worker, Feb. '82.
Teachers' Action – *Police, Propaganda and Pedagogy,* No. 14, Spring, '81.
Issues in Race and Education, *Fishing at Playtime,* No. 29, *Silence is Violence,* No. 31, *Brixton, an Educational Issue,* No. 32.
10 Issues in Race and Education – *Police Force the Issues,* No. 36, Summer '82.
11 ILEA, *Race Sex and Class,* (1) *Achievement in Schools;* (2) *Multi-Ethnic Education in Schools;* (3) *A Policy for Equality : Race;* (4) *Anti-racist statement and guidelines;* (5) *Multi-ethnic Education in Further, Higher and Community Education,* 1983.
12 ILEA Circular 81/133 *Police Entry to School Premises*
13 Advisory Centre for Education, *Police in Schools – Education or Surveillance?* in WHERE to find out more about education, No. 190 July/August 1983.

THE IRISH IN BRITAIN

Cass Breen & Mary Hickman
(Both are members of the Irish in Britain Representation Group.)

The Irish in Britain have generally been ignored in the mushrooming 'race relations industry' of the past decade. Educationalists amongst others have been responsible for the marginalization of the Irish in this context. Many implicitly assume that the Irish have now assimilated. This entails some acknowledgement that the Irish have experienced discrimination and prejudice but this is thought to be a thing of the past. The declining impact of religious hostility and in recent years their white skin colour, are cited to illustrate that the Irish are an example of successful integration. However, the appropriate question concerning the Irish is not 'have they or have they not assimilated' with its implicit assumption that the answer will determine whether they are a problem or not. It is: what can be done about the endemic racism of the British against the Irish? The presumption must be that it is the British who are the problem.

Recently, growing recognition of the Irish has taken the form of locating them as an 'ethnic minority'. Thus they are identified as one of a number of minority groups with a distinctive cultural tradition and a right to perpetuate that within a pluralist framework. The same applies equally to the Asian and Afro-Caribbean groups and to other sizeable minorities e.g. the Vietnamese, Poles and Italians. To categorize together in this manner the different experiences of these minorities in British society is woefully inadequate. It reveals a presumption that it is only uninformed British insularity that causes the hostility and difficulties which such groups encounter.

This multi-cultural approach has come under attack, especially from many Black groups. We too are opposed to it. Some educationalists have also been concerned to distance themselves from its analysis. For example, a paper published by the Berkshire Department of Education, *Education for Equality* draws a clear distinction between Black groups and ethnic minorities on the basis that the former:

> 'have a distinctive historical relationship with Europe'
> 'have distinctive experiences and concerns in Britain at the present time'
> 'and in particular they experience racism'.

The term ethnic minority is rejected as inappropriate to label Black groups because it focuses solely on cultural difference, whereas what demarcates them in Britain is the racism they experience and the colonial legacies which underpin it. The authors of the Berkshire document therefore outline that what they are concerned with is Black/White relationships in British society. They, thus, reduce those aspects of the situation correctly highlighted in exposing the shortcomings of the 'ethnicminority syndrome' to a question of colour.

Racism has never absolutely required skin colour as an organising principle. It is only necessary to remember the racism of a wide range of 'colours' against Jewish people to realise it is not a pre-requisite. It is true, that most racisms utilise physical characteristics to swell their power. Without question, today in Britain, skin colour is a pivotal mainstay of the constant regeneration of racist practices against Asian and Afro-Caribbean groups. As such 'colour' is central to the analysis of their "distinctive experiences and conerns", but it is not the progenitor of racism.

Neither a multi-culturalist argument nor one that equates racism with Black/White relationships can account for the Irish experience in Britain. The Irish and Black groups in Britain may not share skin colour in common, but they have the same antecedents in that British imperialism exploited and distorted the development of their respective countries. The consequent economic under-development was responsible for their forced migrations to Britain.

The Irish experience is not synonomous with that of the various Black groups but the process of migration and induction into Britain which each has undergone can be understood by conceptualising them all as 'colonial minorities'. To grasp the similarities and dissimilarities between them necessitates examining not only the circumstances of migration and the place each group came to occupy in the division of labour in Britain but also the origin of the migrants and specifics of their incorporation into the British class system. The full dimensions of the institutionalised racist practices which characterize 'internal colonialism' and are the experience of all colonial minority groups will then be apparent. A prime site for such practices being the education system.

Anti Irish Racism and the School Curriculum

Racism against the Irish is not only a structural feature of British society, but has for long been one of the hallmarks of popular British culture. The past fifteen years for example, have provided a catalogue of racist practices concerning the Irish: an avalanche of anti-Irish jokes; the enactment of repressive legislation; the distorted accounts of both Irish history and the current war propagated within schools and through the media; and continuing discrimination in the fields of housing/employment/social security. A major priority of the Irish in Britain Representation Group (IBRG), in combating this racism is to seek transformations in school and college curricula. There is little documentation about either the education of the Irish in Britain or the content of education about the Irish. Here we briefly outline the systematic representations which pass for knowledge about Britain's relationship with Ireland, as revealed in a study of teaching materials used in both history and social studies courses.

When a wide range of history textbooks aimed at students ages 11–16 years were examined for their content on Ireland, charges that they were biased and inadequate were confirmed.[1] As with the histories of all Britain's other colonies, which have been indicted by many, the textbooks focus on Ireland only in terms of its contact with Britain. More to the point, it is primarily a history of when the Irish resisted British rule and of the measures taken to deal with them. For example, the history of Anglo-Irish relations in the seventeenth century is given frequent coverage in the books because the Irish rebelled against British rule three times between 1641 and 1689. The eighteenth century, however, is neglected precisely because the rebellion came in 1798. Also no account of Northern Ireland between 1921 and 1968 appears in any history textbook looked at. Some of the more recently published books that make reference to the war since 1969 sometimes include a couple of sentences referring to the 47-year period. Otherwise Ireland is 'signed off' in 1922 with the acceptance in Dublin of partition. This is because from a British viewpoint the Irish problem is seen as having stabilised and is no longer significant until the late 1960's when another crisis erupts for the British state.

The problem for history students to explain is therefore: why did the Irish rebel against British rule? The reason always supplied is 'religious hostility'. The premise is never that of having to explain why the British were in Ireland in the first place. The latter is presumed to be self-evident: 'for security reasons'. These underlying assumptions shape the presentation of 'The Irish Question' in all the books and materials analysed and ensure that a stereotype image of the Irish is conveyed.

The Irish are consistently shown as 'the problem' in contrast with the 'problem solving' British. The existence of the war in Northern Ireland is directly attributed to the backwardness of the Irish political tradition with its religious sectarianism and reliance on physical force methods. The comparison of course, is with the assumed rationality of British political culture with its hallmarks of religious tolerance and democratic procedures for solving conflict. For example, "In 1969 bitter fighting broke out in the streets of Belfast and other northern towns. British troops were sent in to keep the peace, but long-standing religious differences could not be settled overnight", (R J Cootes (1972) *Britain Since 1700,* Longman Secondary Series), and "Between the two (the Provisional IRA and the UDA and UVF) the British Army has the thankless task of trying to preserve some semblance of peace and order in a society where violence and terrorism have often lead to retaliation". (G W O Woodward (1976) *Divided Island,* Heinemann Educational Books)

The upshot of all this is that the heritage of partition and the many other relics of Britain's past total occupation of Ireland, are never explained. The whole problem is reduced to one of religious antagonisms. The many dimensions of the current crisis and the various social forces involved are seen only in terms of 'warring tribes' who require a British presence to keep them apart and maintain law and order. Effectively precluded is any re-examination of Britain's current role in Northern Ireland. The echoes of this in the mass media's accounts of Northern Ireland are easily observed. It is this general framework of British superiority and Irish inferiority which is at the centre of the racism which is common to all British versions of Irish history and interpretations of the present situation.

There have been some isolated changes in the past couple of years. A few schools have produced their own materials and the Avon Learning Development Unit have produced packs on Ireland which attempt to deal in a different way with e.g. British economic reasons for controlling Ireland and how this was achieved, and with the setting up of the Northern Ireland state. In addition, Irish language and history courses have been launched in some adult education institutes and a few schools. However, these piecemeal measures can in no way counteract the unquestioning transmission of the model of Anglo-Irish relations outlined above which is the activity of most courses. A particular case in point being the Schools Council 13–16 Modern History Project which has been responsible for the increased teaching of Irish history in recent years and in every sense conforms to the stereotypes we have been criticising.

It is for all these reasons that the IBRG has identified the struggle against racism in education as a central issue and is making certain specific demands. In the two years since the organisation started up, different ideas have emerged with regard to how we should project our needs and demands. For example, much work has been set in motion in areas like Leicester to increase the range of Irish studies courses available.

One of our major priorities in London is to pressurise local authorities with regard to:

(a) the inadequacy of multi-culturalism as an approach to racism in education and the urgency of developing an educational policy which meets the needs of all colonial minority groups, and

(b) to adopt an anti-racist strategy enabling changes to be implemented in school and college curricula with regard to:

(i) the teaching of history/social studies/English and the presentation of Ireland and the Irish,

(ii) the books, texts, illustrations and teaching materials used,

(iii) in service/retraining facilities for staff and

(iv) arguing for the above to be implemented in schools and colleges as an authority wide policy and not just in areas where Irish people live and attend schools.

It is also an IBRG priority to demand that the ILEA sets up a Resource and Teaching Centre to cover all aspects of teaching on Ireland. Such a centre would have a brief that covered primary, secondary and further education, and would document via research what is actually going on in schools and colleges.

1 Mary Hickman, *The Problematic Irish* – an analysis of the presentation of Britain's relationship to Ireland in school texts. Msc dissertation. The Polytechnic of the Southbank 1980.

N.B. The authors have asked us to point out that this article was originally written in June 1983. They hope that an updated version will be published soon.

ANTI-RACIST TEACHING: General Principles

Martin Francis

There is no doubt that anyone dipping their toes delicately and tentatively into the waters of multi-cultural education can suddenly find themselves up to their necks in churning waters, lashed by cold winds of realism and threatening clouds of political criticism.

Since multi-cultural education has been under attack many teachers have felt a sense of helplessness and despaired of 'getting it right'. We think it is possible to see a way to move forward through the development of anti-racist teaching but are equally aware that there is no escape from the contradictions and conflicts involved. We have to face up to the conflict and working collectively with other teachers is one way of getting some degree of solidarity.

Ironically, it is the de-politicisation of racism through the development of multi-cultural education that leaves teachers unprepared for the issues of power, patronisation and white racism that emerge when they attempt to put multi-cultural ideas into practice in a racist society. Multi-culturalism often seems to argue that all cultures are equally valuable (ignoring the fact that they are not equally powerful), that knowing more about other cultures automatically makes one more 'tolerant' of them (ignoring the fact that racism can be reinforced when antagonistic people study other cultures), that racism is damaging to all people (ignoring the fact that whites benefit from it in the job queue, the housing queue, the qualifications queue).

It is the same liberal multi-cultural education that has also been criticised by black groups when it appears

Protesting in Soweto 1976

International Defence and Aid Fund, 64 Essex Road, London N1

to proceed from stereotypes of black people to offer a particular sort of education provision focusing on black achievement in sport, music and dance. Children from Africa and all the islands of the West Indies found themselves pushed into steel bands. West Indians were expected to be good at sports and were hauled out of academic lessons to train – the stereotypes of 'rhythmic physically powerful' West Indians were totally compatible with the other stereotypes of 'boisterous' 'resentful of authority' that led many black youths into disruptive units – which then offered them sports and reggae to channel their energy!

The question is; does the rejection of this form of multi-cultural education mean that we give up trying to overhaul the curriculum and educational resources to reflect a less eurocentric view of the world? We argue that anti-racist teaching can co-exist with a more politicised form of multi-cultural education that:

'against the background of a recognition of the existence of many cultures in Britain (which will include music, food, dance, etc) also looks at the history of the struggles of those people against colonialism and imperialism and at world development in terms of the relationship between the First and Third World – out of this will develop anti-racist themes which will mesh with an anti-racist policy in the school which deals effectively with racist incidents and racist attitudes. The school will be encouraging discussion of these and other issues (such as gender and class power relationships) and making links with community struggles.'[1]

Thus anti-racist education is clearly political, raising many issues beyond its immediate brief. A useful way of looking at it is through the categories developed by the Birmingham Education Group in Unpopular Education.[2] They claim that postwar education policy has focused on *access* to the education system and that the debate about educational provision has neglected the *context* in which the provision is made, the *control* of the system, and the *content* of what is taught. We would also argue that theories of learning, models of child development, and teaching methods (and the implicit interlinkings of these) are also important.

The Unpopular Education critique suggesting that there has been an over-concentration on equality of access throws light on some of the current debates. They argue that equal access to a system that in itself perpetuates inequality and remains unchanged is a very limited aim. It is a bit like arguing for equal access to public schools which still perpetuate an elitist philosophy and confer privilege on those that attend them. In that light the Government's scheme to allow more lower middle and working class children into public schools could be seen as increasing equality of access. Obviously this is just tinkering with an unfair system. Looked at in terms of race and gender we can see that arguments for more equal access by black people and women to institutions that support the racial and sexist status quo and maintain a patriarchal and euro-centric curriculum and an elitist and hierarchical structure are limited.

Some groups who have argued for more effective teaching of black and girl pupils accept this limited version of educational reform because they see little chance of the situation itself changing. Multi-cultural studies which are not recognised by Oxbridge and other institutions, or by employers as academically credible areas of study may well be *politically* right from our perspective but not *practically* useful to a black parent who wishes her/his child to do well in the system as it exists now. It is the timeless dilemma of reformist vs revolutionary approaches. If black parents are to take multi-cultural education (in its politicised version) seriously they have to have faith in the ability of the system to undergo radical change. Similarly patriarchical syllabus areas may be undergoing change in the CSE arena with children challenging traditional views of history, science and literature but if their studies are later devalued, precisely because they challenged these views – then the child may have gained in her/his personal knowledge and consciousness but not in chances of higher education.

Thus the dilemmas about access bring us on to examining *context*. If our society is one where patriarchal and eurocentric cultures are valued at the expense of others (and it is) we have to look at how the education system perpetuates this situation and at parts of the system which are beginning to challenge these ideas and at the contradictions in the system which puts those ideas under strain. We also have to look at the overall context in terms of Britain's historical development – the loss of empire and colonies, the decline of industry, increasing government authoritarianism, the attempted revival of 'Victorian ideals', the presence of an 'internal colony' once needed for industrial expansion and now no longer required, and of a female workforce that in a period of unemployment is once again being pushed back into the home.

In such a situation there is a clear distinction between the interests of those in power and those without power. The *control* of the education system becomes important. With its control resting in the hands of those who hold power, it can begin to institutionalise and legitimise the inequalities that already exist – not in a monolithic way or as a conspiracy but as part of the wider political battle between left and right. So anti-racist and anti-sexist education, peace studies, development education are challenged by re-affirmation of the family, post-Falklands patriotism, and other conservative ideals. These battles about content and ideology are of limited relevance while the control of the system rests with central government and the establishment. Indeed they can afford to ghettoise some experiments if they don't threaten the system as a whole. Mrs. Thatcher even felt able to endorse a call for multicultural education during the 1982 election campaign. In this respect, attempts at getting more community control of education are potentially radical if the community itself (which of course is not homogeneous) has an element that maintains a critique of the system in terms of access, context, control and content. Schools and teachers committed to anti-sexist and anti-racist education must, in the light of the above, be making links with the community and discussing these issues.

Where does multi-cultural education fit in here? It can be seen as part of the legitimisation of current inequalities – the presence of black people is sweetened for the white population by the more acceptable and consumable parts of their culture – multicultural restaurants, black tv comedies, black recording hits. The oppositional parts of the culture instead of being linked to inequalities in power, income, and discriminatory racist legislation and white racism, are instead seen as mindless outbursts to be soothed with community-police liaison (not community control of police) backed by short, sharp shocks and YOP schemes. Anti-racist education will recognise and be allied with the oppositional elements of black cultures and make those links. This is where the issue of content of the curriculum is important. Yes, we do have to change the content if we want to challenge the power structure and its ideology but we also have to challenge at a political level those who control the system.

Black children and girls themselves experience all this conflict at first-hand. For them, the limitations of multi-cultural education are clear when the PC who regularly stops and searches their older brother sits in the school hall tapping his feet to the school steel band. Homilies about working hard at school are contradicted by friends with qualifications who can't find work, the supremacy of white males on the school staff expose where the power really lies. A relevant education would take all these problems and make them themselves the subject of study – how they came about, the ways in which they are maintained, attempts that are being made to change them and pupils themselves would begin to organise, backed by the resources of the school, to bring about these changes.

Which brings us to the practical part. The teachers delicately dipping their toes into multi-cultural waters may dash back from the waters edge and pretend there is no problem. In an inner-city multi-racial school the pupils will begin to push her back into the water – in the white hinterland she might be able to close her eyes for a little longer but by neglecting the anti-racist education of her white pupils she will be implicitly supporting the racist status quo. There are no easy solutions – as we said there is an ongoing conflict, a power struggle, which is uncomfortable – but by educating the young in a period of major contradictions we have chosen, albeit unconsciously, to be part of the struggle – on one side or the other. So what can we do? Within each area there are some possible lines of action that we can take – some short-term and some long-term:

Context:
As teachers, school staffs and members of professional associations we have to develop our understanding of the current state of British Society. We must recognise the inequalities that exist and the extent and depth of institutionalised racism and sexism. We have to understand the nature of ideologies that support racism and sexism, and not merely dismiss them as crazy or irrational. We must also examine how these ideologies are translated into commonsense beliefs that can be heard on the top of any bus or in the local pub. This will include things like 'They're taking our jobs', 'Women belong in the home', 'The Irish are all stupid'.

This commonsense knowledge is confirmed day in, day out, by the popular press, tv and radio. We must also become aware of the groups and individuals who are struggling to change those inequalities – this means we have to put ourselves out to buy their journals, attend their meetings and talk to them.

Control:
As we said earlier, the school should link with those in the community who want a greater accountability of the school and particularly those who wish to challenge traditional ideas about education. We have to look at how 'professionalism' cuts us off from parents and community and how the autonomy that we value is pretty thin in comparison with the pressures on us from government, examination boards, HMI's and heads. We will be faced with tremendous dilemmas when the community demands things that we are opposed to – but we have to take up the challenge of justifying our beliefs through debate and dialogue with them.

Content:
We have to seek transformation of the content of education not just at the level of what we do in the classroom but in terms of the 'Aims of the School' and the content of examination syllabi. We'll look in more detail later at an attempt to introduce a relevant content in a primary classroom.

Teaching Method:
Anti-racist and anti-patriarchy ideas will have little credibility if the medium doesn't match the method. We have to find ways of breaking down hierarchies in the classroom based on age, sex, race and class through co-operative learning, establishment of girls groups, etc. Such a teaching method will be based on a model of learning that recognises the ability of even very young children to understand complex ideas, cope with conflict,

and organise the contradictory information they receive into some kind of coherent whole – which will be continually transformed by new information and experiences. It will encourage children to seek their own information and challenge established ideas – including those of the teacher.

Access:
Whilst recognising that equal access is a limited concept as demonstrated by the foregoing – ultimately we need changes in control, content and teaching method that will transform schools as institutions – there are still battles around access that need to be fought. These include issues like anti-black and anti-working class discrimination in the selection procedures of some voluntary schools, the provision of science facilities in girls schools, the examinations that pupils are entered for etc. That there needs to be changes in schools themselves is evidenced by the other side of access – the way pupils are being increasingly siphoned off into special schools, disruptive units, tuition centres or are merely absenting themselves from educational institutions altogether.

March 1st

Editor
Daily Star

Dear sir,

I am writing to you about St saviour in Toxteth the reason why some of the children are being naughty is because the head hits them and they get angry and seek revenge and that's how the school was smashed up and damaged.

Plus some of the children live in poorly Flats and maybe their mum or dad is unemployed so they feel down and think that there is no chance of them getting any jobs when they grow up so they go to school and dont do any work because they think education is rubbish.

I think there should be ~~so~~ black teachers because they are strict and some are strong and can control some of the children.

from Monique

Monique raises the issues (see p.112)

ANTI-RACIST TEACHING: Curricular Practices

Martin Francis

This is all very well in theory you may well be saying, but what can you actually do when faced with a class of primary school pupils that you want to be able to read and write but also begin to understand some of the issues that puzzle them?

The first problem that confronts the teacher, particularly in a classroom or school where there has been a tendency to shy away from tackling 'controversial' issues, is to find ways of establishing an atmosphere in which they can be discussed. The organisation of the classroom, provision of materials and teaching styles are important here. By providing multiracial books, resources in childrens' mother-tongues, anti-sexist display materials, 'alternative' sources of information (e.g. community newspapers), encouraging discussion and collaborative learning you can influence the hidden curriculum so as to create an atmosphere in which anti-racist teaching can take place.

Without this background raising the issue of racism and trying to discuss it will come like a bolt from the blue – something completely different, threatening and accompanied by moral pressure. As we have worked on anti-racist teaching in the ALTARF primary workshop it has become clear that in one sense, we are merely talking about good primary practice – but in another we are talking about radical changes in the organisation of schools, teaching method and content. A content that challenges racism and sexism; that recognises the ability of young children to think through issues themselves; that encourages them to argue, debate and organise; that takes established views and subjects them to rigorous examination – cannot leave unexamined the hierarchical nature of schools, the relationship of the school to the local community. Possibly 'good progressive education' meant that anyway – but the sharper edge we are giving it cannot leave the school unscathed.

The progressive axiom of 'starting where the kids are', from their own experience, can be limited to starting a project on metamorphosis where a child brings in a caterpillar but can be extended to include Unpopular Education's idea of making the contradictions children experience themselves the object of study. Over the past few years children have raised with me issues about sexism, racism, local housing, lead in petrol, the powerlessness of young people, unemployment and the nuclear bomb. These issues increasingly impinge on their world as they reach the age of 11 and we will be failing the children if we do not take them up. One of our first tasks is to 'take the lid off' this experience.

To successfully 'take the lid off' the teacher has to have generated the kind of atmosphere in the classroom where children feel free to talk about their experiences, to express strong points of view, and feel able to disagree with each other and the teacher. The way the contradictions of modern society touch the children is often deeply personal and they have to be confident that they will be heard and taken seriously. This is not just a matter of the teacher's attitudes but the child knowing that the teacher or the school has taken on such issues in the past. Building up such an atmosphere is a slow process that goes backwards as well as forwards – particularly when the teacher her/himself is constrained by the school timetable, expectations of other staff, fear of a parental backlash. However, the primary school teacher with the close relationship she/he can develop with the class is in a better position than most.

When you have taken the lid off, you'll probably recoil at what you find – there will be all sorts of attitudes and ideas that will appear prejudiced, reactionary or just plain daft (not that such ideas are absent in teachers . . .) but there will be other ideas that'll emerge when you get down to discussion, that are generous, thoughtful, open-minded, sorted out. You now have the job of sorting out what kind of intervention you can make. You have on your side that it is *contradictions* you are looking at – the views of different children will contradict each other but they will also have individually within themselves contradictory views and interpretations of their experience. The children are involved in a continuous process of building up a picture of their world – feeding into that all sorts of disparate information and experience culled from friends, family, television, comics, books and school. You as a teacher can provide information and experience that can help them clarify things for themselves.

I have looked elsewhere[3] at the various approaches you can take in terms of concentric circles with the child's *personal* experience at the centre, moving out to *school*, the *community*, *national* events, *historical* events, *geographically* distanced events and perhaps even to totally *imagined* starting points. In a sense we can start anywhere in this pattern. In a school with an ethnic minority population the personal may be the best starting point. In an all-white school, national, historical and geographical starting points may be the wisest. The teacher's experience and confidence in raising the issue are also important and those just embarking on this approach may be happiest with the more distanced starting points.

Although in this article I am looking mainly at the anti-racist dimension I will also be looking at examples of anti-sexist and class/community issues. The concentric circles can be applied to all three areas.

Personal Experience
This is where you really 'take the lid off' and get children to talk about their own experience. Getting children to listen to their peers as others they can learn from is very important. They will often shut-up for the authority figure (the teacher) but not for each other. I have found one way of getting over this is to sit in a circle and pass a stone around. You are only allowed to speak when you have the stone. Normally, the stone is passed clockwise or anti-clockwise so that all have a chance to speak. Other teachers have found this artificial and have a system where the stone is passed to anyone who wants it. The first way can certainly enable children to listen to each other and sometimes enables them to get beyond just talking off the top of their head. They have time to consider what they are going to say whilst waiting for the stone to come round. As far as possible the teacher should stick to the rules and not speak 'out of the stone'. If the stone method does not cut out male dominance the group can be split into girls and boys and two groups run and this can also be done with larger classes.

I have tried to develop a tradition of discussion in the classroom so that a racist or sexist remark can be discussed in a setting which has become normal and comfortable – if discussion becomes merely a disciplinary device to deal with such remarks it loses its educative function.

In these discussions I do not see myself as 'neutral' but express my own point of view. Again where there is a tradition of disagreement and challenging, this shouldn't be a problem, although you cannot completely get away from the authority of the teacher. As I listen to tapes of my own classroom discussions I am very aware of how often I am called 'Sir' and how much is directed at me. There will always be something that pupils will profoundly disagree with you about, so that if you get a feeling that they're waiting to 'please the teacher' with the 'right line' you pick a topic on which you're likely to disagree with most of the class. For me these have included Charles' and Di's wedding (their reaction – Aaaaah . . . , mine – Ugh!) and TV (they wanted more, I wanted less). It's important for teacher and pupil that the views you put forward are genuine.

Once pupils have got used to discussion and listening to each other it is possible to have less structured discussions, split into smaller groups or develop techniques of 'reporting back'. This is a transcript of a discussion I had with a small group about a racist name-calling incident. Kim had called John a racist name and following an after school discussion with me had written a letter of apology:

John : Usually when it happens (being called a name) you just want to get the person that said it, really.

Me : You were really angry, and shaking and crying weren't you?

Kim : It weren't really only me that said it, it was Cheryl as well but Cheryl got out of it so that I got all the blame.

Me : But what do you feel about the way we dealt with that, was it better or not?

John : That's the best way to deal with it really. Have a talk with each child and see what you can do and when you can see which one is right or which wrong let that person who is wrong say they're sorry or whatever . . .

Me : Kim, do you really think you were wrong that time?

Kim : Yea.

Me : And what did you think when you wrote the letter to John. Did you *feel* that or were you just doing it because you were told to?

Kim : I weren't doing it because I was told to. I shouldn't have done it in the first place.

Me : What did you think John when you got the letter back?

John : Yes, it's alright but usually you can't take an apology for a few minutes can you? It sticks in your mind . . . usually you don't like taking a letter you like hearing it personally. Like when Kim gave me the letter I made her read it all out to me and say it first.

Lorraine : You know when you tell teachers something, like if you had a fight, they look at you as if they don't know you, as if you came from Mars or Jupiter or something.

John : Yes, like you're an outerspacer, like they've never seen you before.[4]

Later in the discussion I asked John if teachers tried to understand what was happening to children:

John : No, not really, they just deal with school and the rest of it's nothing to do with them.

The 'rest of it' is to do with racism in the community outside, the experience of being black, linking up with all the concentric circles I've outlined. It is also to do with the experience of being white and under pressure from racists:

Paul : In some schools I've heard about, if some white kids don't want to joint the NF, the NF beat them up. If they tell about what they're doing to the black people they make the white people join NF.

Jack : When I tried to leave the NF they beat me up for no reason. They always do that . . . They were too much violent and they were just beating up people and stabbing them and all that. They just started beating me up. They were calling me 'chicken' and 'nigger lover' and all that.

In such discussions it's not just heavy issues like that which come through but more positive ones where white children can hear black children expressing strong feelings about their language and culture:

Michael : I will teach my children (patois). If someone comes up and speaks to my children in our language, I'll teach them our language so that they can say something back to them.

Me : Do you enjoy speaking patois?

Michael : Yes, it's nice. Because of the kind of accent you speak in.

Me : Do you feel different when you're speaking patois, to when you're speaking English?

Michael : It's as though I'm in a different world when I'm speaking it.

From an anti-sexist viewpoint such discussions often centre on being called names such as cissy or tomboy, but also of feelings and behaviour. Here again, the teacher is crucial and we *all* have our own direct experience to throw into the discussion. As a male teacher I'll take a group of boys while a female colleague takes the girls. You have to be prepared to sit down and be open – to talk about your own childhood and the kinds of fears and misconceptions you had and also about how often you cry, what you are still scared of. Lifting the lid off in this way reveals a whole can of worms. Such discussions and follow-up lessons form the background to Wendy's account (page 162) of the taking up of sexist comments by boys in the class.

If children are going to be as open and revealing about themselves as these quotations imply it's clear that the school has to reciprocate by taking up the issues they raise. Such discussions are often painful (for different reasons) for both black and white children, and for both girls and boys. It would be a gross misuse of the trust placed in us if we took no action about them or see the discussions as ends in themselves.

School

Apart from pupil-pupil and staff-pupil relationships there are also school based issues of curriculum and resources. Multi-cultural and anti-racist education can sometimes get it wrong. The emphasis on slavery for example can push black people into the victim role, liberated by a white knight (Wilberforce, praised so wholeheartedly by the establishment recently and credited with the abolition of slavery by Mrs Thatcher) and not recognising the struggle of black people themselves. The following extract shows that an attempt to get beyond that still has problems:

Me : So what do you think about some of the things we've done? Have you enjoyed . . . we've done a bit about Paul Robeson and Harriet Tubman . . .?

Michael : . . . and Olaudah Equiano . . .

Jackie : . . . and Toussaint L'ouverture.

Me : Did you talk to your parents about doing that sort of history?

Jean : I did.

Michael : I've talked about that. They said they don't like people giving us that kind of history in that way. Because you never find them giving King Henry history in that way, like King Henry had to work on plantations and black people whipping him. They wouldn't give a history in that way. They only give it in coloured pęoples way wouldn't they?

Me : How should it be taught then?

Michael : It should be taught in the same way white people's history is taught.

Me : But you can't change what happened can you?

Michael : No, but there's still some history of black people hidden in the past but they don't want to record it . . . I'm sure that there's a lot of black history but they don't want to record it . . . I'm sure that there's a lot of black history but they don't want us to know about it. They only let us know about King Henry who was white and all those things.

Jackie : Because if they did they think we might want to start it (the fight against white oppression?) again.

That conversation made me think about what I was doing and it's salutary to check up on yourself in this way. It seemed that despite my attempts, the image of slavery: plantation workers, whippings, was still the main one getting through. This is an important aspect of what happened but not the only one. This image was compounded at the time by the screening of the TV film *Roots* that aroused mixed feelings among black pupils in the class. I'll be dealing later in more detail with the use of history in anti-racist teaching.

The resources of the school are also important and convey messages to children about the school's attitudes towards black peoples' presence in Britain and towards black pupils:

Mary : In the books they show more white people and in the advertisements.

Ann : Like we're not there. Like we're nothing.

Echoes of Lorraine and John feeling treated like 'outerspacers'!

Apart from the absence of black people in books there is also the question of how they are portrayed when they are present. In ALTARF's BBC2 Open Door Programme, *Racism the 4th R*[5] we showed Mara Chrystie taking up the issue of illustrations in the Dinosaur book *Going Swimming* with her class of infants. A child had objected to black people being coloured in grey in the pictures and the class decided to write to the author:

'Dear Jill,

I like the story but I don't like the pictures 'cos people are really brown and no people are really grey. When I go out in the street I don't see any grey people. I am a bit white and bit brown . . .'

The publishers were hurt because they thought they were being accused of being racist, while others thought the issue was trivial. In fact it showed several fundamental aspects of anti-racist teaching: the teacher took the issue up after a child had raised it (i.e. it was not dreamed up by over-sensitive, trendy teachers); the children made their own alternative book (demystifying books and showing the illustrations could be better) and the children were encouraged to see that their views were legitimate and to take action about them (writing to the author and publisher). The item shows that children can from a very early age be encouraged to be critical of learning materials and that even well-meaning publishers (Althea have an anti-racist policy) and schools (the books had gone through a screening process for racist/sexist content) can get it wrong.

Similarly I was pulled up by one of the pupils in my class last year. I am in charge of library and resources at my school and prided myself that I'd tried to get some good anti-racist and anti-sexist books in. However, Wendy said different:

"Well, I think there isn't enough black books in school. They've got *Peter and Jane* and they're white and they haven't got any books for black kids and if they have they're just silly books – they're not sensible."

In fact we don't any longer have the Ladybird reading scheme but use the Moon Individualised system to draw on a wide range of multi-racial books. However, the remark about the black books being silly seemed to reflect a feeling that they failed to address the issue of racism – they were humorous or, like *Berron's Tooth,* cosy. Again we do have books that address racism – mainly fiction for older Juniors but Wendy and her friends wanted something different:

"... So what we tried to do (which we never finished) we made up our own book after a programme about people getting jobs and racism. We did a book about jobs and drew pictures and we talked about why black people hadn't been getting jobs. Was it because of their colour or is it just because they're not qualified and we got to the decision that it was because of their colour. So what we did was we got together, we had a discussion before we started making the book, and we just started writing it down and drawing pictures about it."

The fact that 10 and 11 year olds wanted a book that confronted contemporary racism in a factual way, reveals not only their own political understanding but the under-assessment of their ability to understand, made by both teachers and publishers.

Obviously books should also be looked at in terms of sexist bias but school issues go much wider. I surveyed my class and asked them questions about the suitability of books in the class for boys and girls, whether topics chosen for class study were generally orientated to boys' or girls' interests, whether I as a teacher spent more time with boys or girls, whether boys or girls were more often the cause of disruption in the class, whether the cleverest pupil in the class was a boy or girl. The answers to the questions were not only informative to me as a teacher apart from girls' general satisfaction with books and the cleverest child nominated by both boys and girls being a girl they revealed a perception by both girls and boys of sexist bias) they formed the basis of a very full class discussion. This resulted in being able to refer to the survey, and the discussion, when particular boys were being a nuisance later as well as looking at books and topics with more care.

The school structure itself can become the subject of study. Using a video camera borrowed from the local Teachers Centre I did a project on jobs with 1st and 2nd year Juniors. We interviewed various workers in the school: teacher (male), secretary (female), cook (female). The children worked in groups to prepare the questions and then these were pooled and the final list decided and allocated between the children. Informed by discussions we'd had about housework and male and female roles within that, and pay and promotion the children asked not just about the job but about the effects on home life. Did the female workers' husbands share the housework, was it equal? They also asked about pay and whether the jobs paid enough. As a background to the project we had a wall display on jobs which asked pertinent questions about school. Why do boys and girls line up separately? Why don't we have a woman school-keeper? Why don't we have male dinner helpers? Similarly questions can be asked about the proportion of black workers in the school and one child asked the (black) nurse about whether her colour had made it harder to get a job.

Sometimes support from outside can be important in raising the issues in school. Theatre Kit produced a Girls Project about 2 years ago. The show dealt with sexist stereotypes through sketches and pupils' participation and produced a strong sense of identity amongst the girls. The show was for girls only and that in itself was challenging for male staff and male pupils. Boys hung around the hall trying to see what was happening and male teachers were shooed off by girl pupils. The boys were quite threatened at something for girls only (despite their football etc being a mainly boys only activity). I had a discussion with the boys while the girls were attending the Girls Project about why the play was a Girls Only event and got onto wider discussion about sexism and sexuality. The girls came out from the show shouting slogans of 'Girls are

Powerful' and were on a real high for several days. As a result girls formed their own Girls Group and held discussions in the school library at lunchtimes but had problems with harassment from other pupils, particularly boys. This caused discipline problems and as Wendy explains in her interview they were thrown out and we had to eventually make space for their discussions during ordinary classtime. Obviously my role as a male teacher with the group was extremely limited but I was able to invite a friend who is a feminist and interested in working with girls to come in occasionally to work with them while I worked with the boys.

It would be silly to pretend that such activities do not present problems for a school. They raise questions about staff-pupil relationships, teaching style and democracy and may well be opposed by some staff (teaching and non-teaching) who are happier with the old structures and relationships. They may also be opposed by others who see them as pseudo-democratic and a 'progressive cover' on structures and relationships that remain fundamentally unchanged. I would argue that there is space available to undertake some of these activities and that the pupils themselves will begin to work out whether they are a con. It only took 2 months for one pupil to return to school and denounce the School Council that she'd got involved with at her new secondary school.

Community

The relationship between the school and its local community is a vital aspect of this teaching approach. Rather than being separated from the locality, a little island, school should be involved in the community and the community in the school. Obviously one can have a long argument about the very concept of community – the lack of homogeneity in real localities, decisions about who you feel represents the community etc. However those issues will come up anyway once the school gets involved in community issues and are better answered through practice than through theoretical discussion. In any school locality there will be issues and pressure groups that are known to the pupils and the staff who live in the area. Wendy's project on racism was stimulated by a video I showed the class of a BBC2 Brasstacks programme on racism and employment. To bridge the gap between a national programme about Birmingham and our own locality I invited two workers in from the local Black Information Unit to talk about their work in the unit with the class. The discussion ranged from discussions about specific examples of racism in employment and housing brought up by the pupils to a general discussion about education and its value. The session was very rewarding and demonstrated to the children that a local group was taking up the issues raised by the TV programme.

Environmental Studies has a large part to play in anti-racist teaching. As part of a project about pollution we made a tape-slide programme about the Clem Attlee Estate just opposite the school. The slides covered the usual problems of litter, dogs' muck and vandalism but also looked at the large amount of racist graffiti on the Estate (since painted out). The children recorded a discussion about the graffiti and the feelings it aroused and the tape-slide programme was shown to the whole school in assembly. When we made a visit to Chelsea Football Club we discussed the problem of NF fans with the person who showed us around. She told the children that the club was concerned about it and was trying to stop the distribution of literature and display of flags in the ground. Now that the club has black players the manager has received several threatening razor blade letters so this is still very much an issue. After seeing the large amount of graffiti on benches in Bishops Park, we contacted the local council to ask them to get it removed.

Both within the Environmental Studies Group and

the class generally we have had several discussions about housing and racism. We have discussed whether some local estates are being used as dumping grounds for black families, a builder's rcmark to one boy that the houses he was building 'weren't for blacks', a white child's description of her street where the whites lived in the newer houses with gardens while the blacks lived in older properties without gardens. The children, coming as they do from different sorts of housing, also discussed the advantages of highrise and older terraced housing and the relative merits of council, housing association and private property. It would be useful later to get in somebody to speak about Housing Co-ops as another alternative. Within such discussions there was always a thread about racism but the question of housing for single-parent families wasn't adequately discussed and perhaps a future project would benefit from a speaker from Gingerbread. Similarly Threshold or a similar agency could help with looking at housing for single people.

As I said earlier anti-racist education forms part of a wider educational approach. Racism comes up in community issues but conflicts over local resources can produce a united approach. This happened over the Fulham Baths campaign that took place some years ago[6]. There was a big campaign to save the baths in which many children took part. We discussed the issue at school, basing it on evidence from local newspapers and the broadsheet produced by the S.O.B. (Save Our Baths) Campaign. The baths had two swimming pools, slipper baths and a laundry. We did some role-play in which pensioners and children took on a cost-cutting councillor. The children got really interested and we spent an art lesson making Save Our Baths posters and a language lesson writing open letters to the council arguing the case for saving the Baths. We went on to discuss how these could be used usefully and decided to take them down to the Baths for the workers to use.

Martin Francis

Save Our Baths

They were displayed outside the building when the Baths were eventually occupied by local people.

We should not ignore local councils which are the first layer (after schools) of political structure that children encounter. Environmental Studies raises many political issues, some of which are dealt with by planners and councillors at the local town hall. We are lucky in having an Urban Studies Centre in Hammersmith (which has recently gained independent status) which is a great help but even where this doesn't exist you can make your own contacts. Having spent a term doing Environmental Studies with one small group I invited the newly re-elected local councillor to a discussion with the children. We'd had our own mock election in which issues of housing and jobs had been debated and they were well prepared for her. They raised questions about more Council help for setting up factories and workshops to provide jobs in the area and asked about the housing issues described above. Some girls, annoyed that there was a Boy's Club on their estate but no provision for girls, argued for a Girl's Club. This wasn't just PR for the councillor – some of them had lobbied before and had got nowhere, so were sceptical:

Sean: Me and my brother, and all our other mates wanted a club and we went on a march with banners and all these public people started joining in . . . (the councillor advised him to get a petition together which she'd present to the Council) . . . one time we did go to this big, big, building and it had this big round table and my mum came and my brother and sister, and all the other people and we sat down and we started talking about why we wanted a club and everything but we didn't get one.

What happens to such campaigns is itself politically educational. The Save Our Baths Campaign and Sean both lost – but the children were able to get a local football pitch opened up after petitioning the Council.

National

Children are very aware of their political powerlessness. This comes up when they discuss what they can do about major issues. After discussing the nuclear bomb, one class went through several stages – first they would write to Reagan and Thatcher and then decided that they "wouldn't take any notice of us kids because we're too young", then they decided to lie about their ages and pretend they were aged 16 or 18, then they decided they would take no notice anyway. Interestingly, one child observed after a discussion about whether children should have the vote, "We should have the vote. I hope we don't have to throw ourselves in front of the King's horse again like somebody else did."

Children can readily identify with other children – particularly because of this sense of powerlessness, which goes along with other childhood oppressions: lack of money, being described as childish, being excluded from adult conversation, denial of child sexuality. Drama and creative writing are both areas where this identification can be strongest. One national issue that we took up was the so-called St. Saviours School riot. The Toxteth Primary School was in the headlines of all the popular newspapers. Lurid stories blamed one particular black girl, Sharon, for what took place. We started by comparing the accounts in the *T.E.S.* and the *Sunday Times* with the tabloid newspapers. We saw the stereotype of the 'big, black bully' described in the *Sun* and *Star*, challenged by the *Sunday Times'* description of a hard-working, fairly academic, but 'stroppy' black girl. We discussed what made people stroppy and then looked at an account of an argument that preceded the riot when it was claimed that the school cook had called Sharon 'black bastard'. We discussed the whole issue of racist abuse. We then broke down into groups and the children acted out parts of the 'story'. They decided themselves who was to play which part and in two groups a white child played Sharon. One scene gave the children the experience of what it is like to be 'set on' by the press. Sharon and her mum were beseiged by reporters and the children playing the parts really did end up bewildered and saying things that they did not intend to say.

The drama itself may seem crude but the discussion afterwards raised issues about the estate St. Saviours served, about the complaints that had been made about the school to the local black community centre, about the fact that none of the teachers lived in the area, and about corporal punishment. Just in case anyone thinks this is all indoctrination, when we came to write letters to the *Daily Star* in conclusion, quite a few children retained a view that what had happened was 'disgusting' and felt Sharon should be caned. However, Monique had a wider view:

"The reason why some of the children are being naughty is because the head hits them and they get angry and seek revenge and that's how the school was smashed up and damaged. Plus some of the children live in poorly flats and maybe their mum or dad is unemployed so they feel down and think that there is no chance of them getting any jobs when they grow up so they go to school and don't do any work because they think education is rubbish."

Safina said:

"I think that corporal punishment should be abolished, because this does not improve the student's behaviour but makes it even worse. They become more aggressive and revolting in their attitudes. This spoils the relation with teachers and just wastes the students' and teachers' time and government's money . . . the students will be more attentive and will progress better in friendly, understanding surroundings."

Eventually we decided not to send the letters to the

Star as we weren't sure how they'd be used and what reaction there would be to them.

National and local issues were compared when we looked at press coverage of the New Cross Fire march and local coverage of a 'riot' after a Chelsea football match. The former talked about 'mobs' of black youths smashing windows, etc., towards the end of the march – put into perspective it was only a tiny proportion of the march which was otherwise peaceful. The latter involved fans calling out racist taunts and the black staff of Fulham Broadway Underground Station having to lock themselves in to protect themselves. A police spokesman described the fans as 'boisterous' and the situation as under control. Some of the children had been around the area at the time and could compare their observations with what the newspaper said.

Historical

Historically one can look at black heroes and heroines and this was the approach adopted by ILEA's Learning Materials Service which has published various biographies. As the extract printed under the 'personal' section shows this is an approach I have used. Toussaint L'Ouverture, Marcus Garvey, Olaudah Equiano, Paul Robeson and Martin Luther King all make good subjects but the area can be expanded by bringing in the connections between the black and women's movement. *Women, Race and Class* by Angela Davis[7] is an invaluable source for information on women such as Sojourner Truth and Mary Church Terrell. Such a study apart from showing black women fighting on both fronts will also be able to show the part white women played in them as Angela Davis states:

"When Mary Talbert and her Anti-Lynching Crusaders reached out to white women, they felt that white women could more readily identify with the

Black cause by virtue of their own oppression as women."

When I have done work on Mary Seacole and Harriet Tubman I have always had a good response from children. I remember years ago in Paddington when I did my first lesson on Harriet Tubman, a black girl saying, "I never realised black women could be famous".

Alongside this however, there needs to be developed some understanding of the relationship between Britain and the former colonies, of colonialism and imperialism – the relationship summed up in the phrase 'we are here because you were there'. A visit we made to the Asante exhibition at the Museum of Mankind, not only showed children a little of the craftmanship (sic) and social structure of that kingdom, but also led to a discussion of the role of Britain in the break-up of the Kingdom and one pupil talking to us about his Asante grandmother. It is also possible, using the War on Want material, to do work on trade relationships using their information on the banana trade with Dominica. There is a very effective exercise that you can do which shows how much of the money paid for bananas eventually gets back to the producer. The discussion with the local councillor led to debate about whether it was better to pay more rates and get good services. The banana exercise can lead to a discussion about how more money could get back to the real producers of the goods we get from abroad and whether we should pay more, or cut out the profit of the importers etc.

We also need to make connections between Nazism and present day right-wing groups. Children ought to know what Nazism did and also that there are groups in this country sympathetic to their aims. The ITV programme 'How We Used to Live' covering 1936-1953 is useful here. It is played against the background of the rise of Hitler and includes scenes showing Blackshirt activity. One of the girls at the centre of the story has a Jewish friend who lives next door, who becomes increasingly apprehensive as events develop and eventually goes to America. The children's version of *Anne Frank's Diary* can be read to the class and some teachers have found the story *I am David*[8] also useful. It is essential that we take up issues of anti-semitism, particularly as I for one have noticed an increase in anti-semitic remarks and the use of Jew/Jewish as an insult recently. There is also a need to tackle anti-Irish prejudice and this is an area which I hope ALTARF will be able to work on – it connects up with colonialism at a general level but also directly with children's culture in the whole area of Irish jokes.

The series 'How We Used to Live' (1936-53) is also useful for looking at Women at Work and the whole area of women doing 'men's' jobs during the Second World War. There is one telling scene at the end of the war when the mother of the family in the film, who is a school teacher hears a radio broadcast. It is a news item saying that women teachers will not get equal pay with male colleagues and a statement by a teachers' union saying that the nation is in danger of producing a generation of effeminate boys because of the preponderance of women in the profession! Plenty of scope for discussion there. Children's grandparents and older members of the teaching and non-teaching staff are an excellent primary source of information for work in this area.

There isn't really enough space to go on with any more examples, but an effort should be made to introduce a black perspective into the history that we do. Chris Power's book on *Black Settlers in Britain*[9] is an excellent source of information. At other times we have to do our own research and develop our own resources. Doing a project on the Second World War in a school with about 50% West Indian children, I realised that we were ignoring black people's participation in the War. This was corrected by using the parents of the children as a resource and making contact with an older West Indian who tape-recorded an account of West Indians leaving the island to join the British forces and the collecting of scrap metal and money which contributed to three battleships. Such information is a necessary balance – particularly when one of the first cries of the racist is, 'I fought for this country in the war and . . .'

Geographical

A distance is provided by using examples from other countries and at the same time develops an international perspective which links various areas and levels of struggle. Too often material about South Africa produces an 'abject victim' image – something that seemed to be there in the recent competition (!) winner for poems about what it is like to black in South Africa. This is not to deny suffering but to say that we should also stress the struggle that is being waged by black and coloured people themselves in South Africa. Winnie Mandela is a magnificent example to children and someone they should learn about. There is also the example of South African school children themselves.

Using that radical source the *Times Educational Supplement*, we looked at the school students revolt in South Africa and the demands that they were making. The children were shocked by the statistics on educational expenditure and the remarks that were made by government spokesmen but admired the stand that the school pupils were making.

I asked for their reaction:

Saul: (who is white) It's good that they're trying to do something.

John: They'll be noticed. The government will see how much they've been dejected. They'll be worried.

Me : If you were there, what would you be doing about it?

John : Striking with them! (chorus of agreement)

The discussion that took place towards the end of the lesson connected up lots of issues back through our concentric circles. One of the children compared the pass laws with sus and another talked about what changes she'd like to see in our school. Another child referred back to a lesson we'd done on the Burston School Strike. The fact that teachers had been sacked for sympathising with the school students and that the students had themselves demanded the sacking of others invited discussion about teachers and racist attitudes. In a sense you can't separate the issues and again and again I find that even with the most distanced subjects the children themselves make connections.

Imagined

I don't know if this title is really the most apt. What I'm talking about is presenting children with an artificial situation which has the educational aim of bringing out some of the issues we're dealing with. I suppose the 'Eye of the Storm' exercise of treating children differentially, according to the colour of their eyes – which aims to teach them about racism, qualifies for this section. It's not something I've ever done and feel a little unhappy about – mainly because I don't like to pull the wool over kids' eyes. They can be involved in an imaginative exercise and know that it is artificial and still get something from it.

One particular exercise that left a lasting impression on me was when I was working with a woman colleague on sex roles. We presented the children with this scenario: there had been a nuclear war and the earth was devastated and polluted. It was necessary to leave the planet. Two planets were available and as women felt that men's aggression had caused war in the first place they were going to their own planet. Men, with little choice were going to another. The class was then split into the two groups and the boys worked with me in one room, and the girls with the woman teacher in another. Our task was to decide how our planet was to be organised, how we would feed ourselves, house ourselves, whether we would industrialise, who would do what tasks, how children would be reared and educated. Plus: we were to present a sketch to show how we did all those things – (we had test-tube babies).

The lesson took all afternoon. The boys discussed how to govern themselves – first they went for democracy and that didn't work (their leaders couldn't make decisions), then they went for dicatorship (but didn't like being bossed around). Lastly, they split into two warring factions, one of which started to try and farm, but had to build an army to defend itself from marauders from the other side. In order to build arms they had to industrialise – the rearing of children, agricultures and housework were forgotten in the 'war' that they were fighting.

The girls on the other hand, sat in a circle and discussed what they were going to do. They decided to live in a village with the houses all facing a green but with individual living quarters. They farmed, houseworked and child-reared according to a rota. They decided not to industrialise to any great extent because that might lead to more war, pollution and anyway they didn't want to work in factories.

You can imagine the discussion that took place afterwards and the kinds of lessons we drew from the boys' lack of co-operation. Something that some of them had strived to overcome against all the odds and ended up angry and frustrated.

A similar lesson was done when the Government booklet on nuclear survival, *Protect and Survive* was first published. We imagined that war was imminent and eventually a bomb was dropped on Heathrow. We followed the instructions in the booklet and built our own shelter. This involved moving tables to the centre of the room, taking off the doors of the classroom and cupboards, and emptying bookshelves to use books as the walls of the shelter. We used the stipulated signal to say that a bomb had dropped and the children had had enough after about half an hour in the shelter. The exercise was upsetting to some of the children, as it became very real to them, although they did of course know it was a drama lesson. It showed them the practical inadequacy of the Government's instructions and they were well aware of how much better off we were at school for materials like tables, doors, and books, than they were themselves at home. A couple of them declared that if there was a bomb warning they would go out in the playground and play a game and die happily rather than be stifled in a shelter.

CONCLUSION

I've tried to show here how some of these issues can be tackled. The approach is not only about content, but also about teaching style and school democracy. It is also about the aims of education. There is no reason why any of this should lead to a reduction in 'standards' – much of it can be done through writing, drama, science, social studies and other areas of the curriculum. Some of the work we did on the press and the St. Saviours 'riot' was done as a comprehension exercise. We have studied allocation of money for rates and the Government's budget as a maths lesson which involves quite complex mathematical skills, including the working out of percentages of large figures. Similarly, we resorted to maths to explain why Mrs Thatcher got fewer votes in the 1982 election but a bigger House of Commons majority. More importantly, this type of educational approach develops the ability to question, argue, debate, seek out information, assess conflicting information and to organise. It is complemented by encouraging the children to use resources such as type-writers, duplicators and video. Yes, it is political – but yes, it is also educational.

1 *ALTARF NEWSLETTER* No. 5, May 1983.
2 *Unpopular Education – Centre for Contemporary Cultural Studies,* Hutchinson, 1981
3 *Cambridge Journal of Education,* Easter 1982
4 These transcripts have been published in part in several publications including Issues in Race and Education, Children and Socialism *(Big Flame)*, and *The Guardian.*
5 *Racism the 4th R,* BBC2/ALTARF. Available on video (VHS format) from ALTARF.
6 For a fuller account see 'Community, Conflict and the Classroom' in *Bulletin of Environmental Education,* June 1982
7 *Women, Race and Class;* Angela Davis – The Women's Press 1981.
8 *Diary of Anne Frank* – Kestrel Books
I am David – Ann Holm, Macmillan Education/Magnet
9 *Black Settlers in Britain,* Nigel File & Chris Power

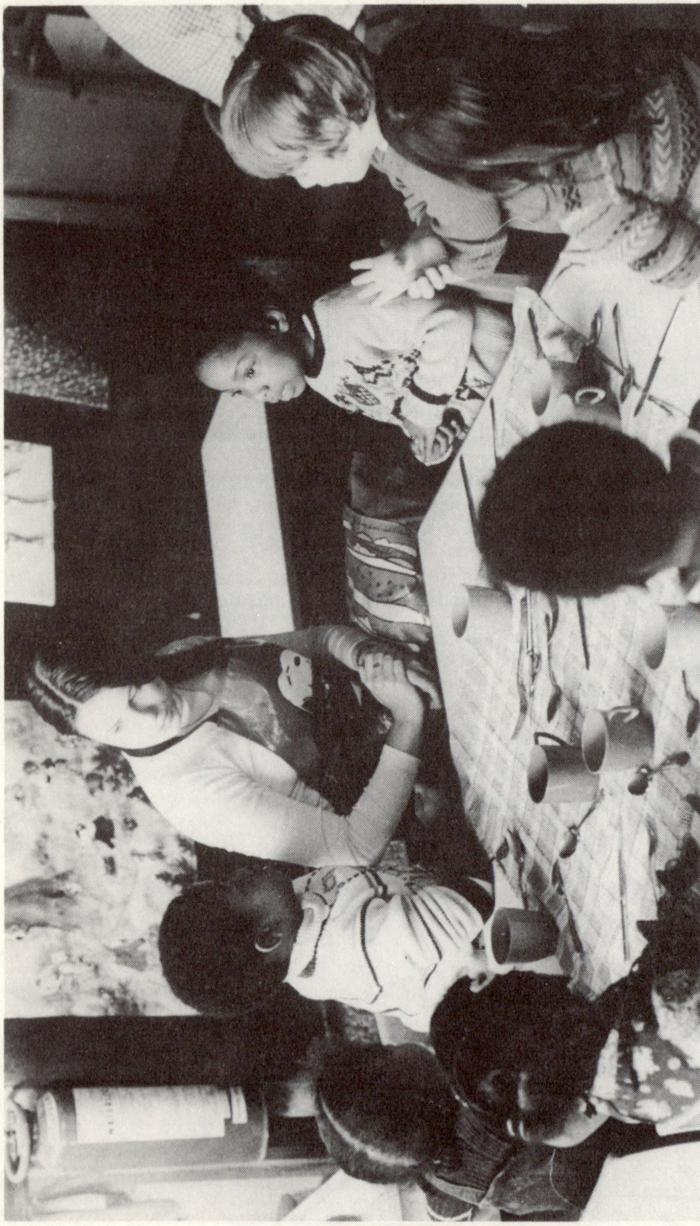

Mark Rusher

ANTI-RACIST NURSERY EDUCATION

Sarah Brimblecombe

Introduction

When ALTARF's booklet on primary education was published we argued that primary teachers were in a unique position to do anti-racist work. The reasons we gave for this: sustained contact with a group of children, close links with parents, a potential for involvement in the local community; can be applied even more strongly to the nursery field.

These articles arose out of early meetings of the ALTARF nursery workshop but already outline a framework for further discussion. It is clear that opportunities for anti-racist education occur at a number of levels:

1. increasing the awareness of nursery staff about the issues
2. discussing the nursery's anti-racist stance with parents
3. making links with the local community
4. creating a multi-cultural and anti-racist environment for the children.

As the nursery may be a parent's (as well as a child's) first experience of an institution that has built into it a series of racist assumptions – and as such will be giving both white and black adults and children lessons about the education system, it is clear that the nursery has to examine very clearly the attitudes of staff, its relationship with parents and community, and the values inherent in the work it does with children. There are other issues that also need fuller examination including the different forms of pre-school provision (play groups, one o'clock clubs, child-minders, day nurseries, nursery classes, nursery schools) and whether they are available on an equal basis to all ethnic groups and whether they answer the needs of those groups; as well as the question of the actual ethnic mix of the staffing of nurseries and their position in the hierarchy.

Multi-cultural playthings and books will not be enough if at the same time racist remarks are ignored, or if a parent encountering racism from neighbours or the police, or facing deportation does not feel able to call upon the nursery for help.

Children do notice colour – What are we going to do about it?

Racist feelings affect everyone; they are part of the world we live in. Racism is one of the major concerns of families whose children are about to start primary school. Families are anxious that their children might be subjected to the expression of racist feelings, or that they may no longer be protected from racist attitudes as they were at home. School is a much larger social world where many views are heard.

This concern of families is something that teachers have to consider. It is a concern that could fundamentally affect their working. Nursery staff, at a stage before children enter the primary school, have to think about ways in which they can help the very young children they are with, look at their racist views.

Research[1] has shown that nursery age children are aware of the colour of the people they meet. They are beginning to code and classify their world. What interpretations are they to put on the group of people who are called 'white' or the group of people who are called 'black'? What is the role of the nursery staff in this process? Do they have a part to play or is it entirely a matter for the child and her/his family?

A family placing a child in a nursery is asking other people to care for the child for a certain period of time. Nursery staff have a certain function to fulfil as carers and educators but they remain individuals with a particular view of life, and that view will necessarily influence the way they work. It may not be the same view as the child's family.

In order to help children sort out the fact that people have different colours and adjust to the idea that they could come from a family which does not act in the same way as her/his own, the nursery staff have really to examine their own feelings about race and cultural diversity. The examination of personal ideas may come about in a variety of ways. It may be an isolated incident in the nursery that can start the process off. It may be a remark devaluing language such as: 'Adnan doesn't talk', when the child concerned is learning English as a second language.

Sometimes children come out with a directly racist remark such as: 'I don't like you, you're black', or 'My mummy says I mustn't play with black kids'.

How should nursery staff respond to these comments given that the response must be at a level the child can understand?

The language issue can be dealt with practically, sometimes by reference to the child's own peer group[3]: 'You listen to Adnan when he is with Nazrul. He does talk. He talks Bengali. It sounds different.'

It can be followed up by making sure that the child who is convinced that Adnan does not talk *hears him talk*.

Where there is mother tongue provision in the nursery, a child who is uncertain about anything other than her/his own language being real talk, will have the opportunity to see adults and children effectively communicating in a new way.

Individual children who say that they don't like someone because they're black or white, can be encouraged to look at their own friendship groups. It is vital that matters are discussed with the parents of any child who has been told not to play with a particular group of children, so as to put the following points:

'What are you really asking the staff to do?'

'Do you mean the children to be segregated?'

It is then for the parents and staff to decide how to resolve the problem. Sometimes, it is a meeting or remarks made outside your work-place which may set off thoughts about racial issues. It is important that nursery staff are able to be sufficiently open with each other to acknowledge racism exists.

In discussing the existence of racism and how you feel about it in connection with young children, it is inevitable that not only who the child plays with, but what the child plays with, will be discussed.

Does the nursery reflect a little of the world we live in? Do the children's books reflect a balance of different cultures? Does the selection of books give an equal value to each of the languages represented in the selection? Does the home corner have a variety of accessories which reflect cultural diversity?

Families provide the best resource available to a nursery committed to reflecting cultural diversity. Going to nursery is primarily a social experience of learning to be with people. It is very important that every person in a nursery class is seen to be valued and enjoyed by everyone else. This means a genuine acceptance of everything a child and her/his family has to offer. This is vital to the child being able to build up a secure and effective model of the world. Children are very sensitive to stereotypes and unexpressed views[4] or actions which might undermine a positive value a nursery is trying to express.

The reasons for the nursery's interest in different cultures must be discussed with the family before the child begins in the nursery so that the family has time to think it over, and to ensure that there is no feeling of the nursery merely paying lip-service to the idea of anti-racist strategies.

It is not always easy to talk about racial issues with people you do not know well. However, everyone has a point of view on the subject and has had some experience of racism. Build on that, choose the moment, and from that build on. We can show children that we enjoy sharing the different cultures of people we meet and that we are also prepared to make a stand against discrimination and unfairness. By our behaviour we can influence the way children see each other.

REFERENCES

1 *Children, Race and Racism,* Louise Derrian Sparks
How Race Awareness Develops, Carol Higa and Bill Sparks
2 *From Mother Tongue to English,* Daphne Brown OUP 1979
3 Racism : the Young Childs Experience in School
4 Pauline France, Centre for Urban Educational Studies 1982

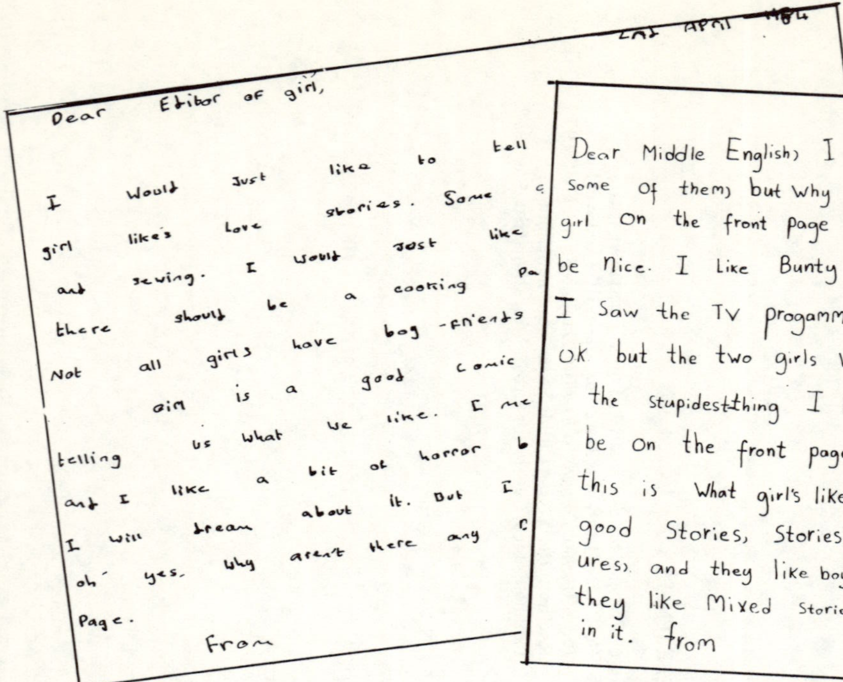
2nd April 1984

Dear Etibor of girl,

I Would Just like to tell
girl like's Love stories. Some c
and sewing. I would Just like
there should be a cooking Pa
Not all girls have boy-friends
girl is a good comic
telling us what we like. I me
and I like a bit of horror b
I will dream about it. But I
oh yes. Why aren't there any C
Page.

From

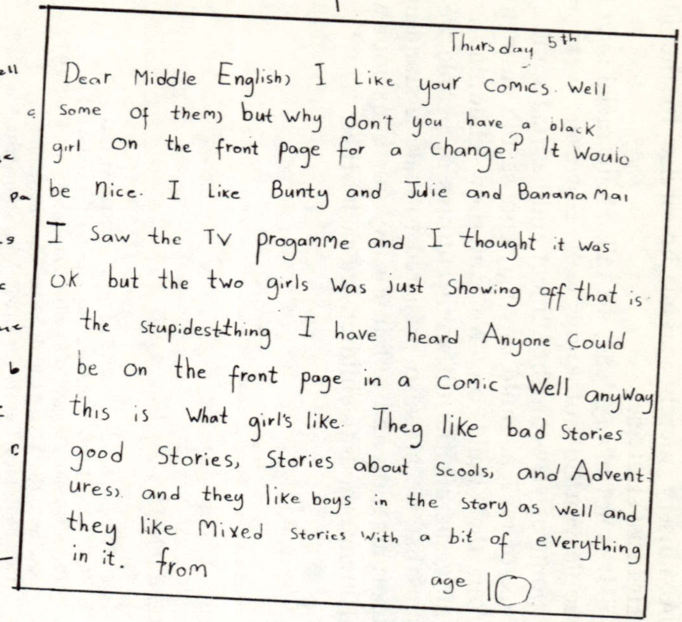
Thursday 5th

Dear Middle English, I Like your Comics. Well Some of them, but why don't you have a black girl On the front page for a Change? It Would be Nice. I Like Bunty and Julie and Banana Mai

I Saw the TV progamme and I thought it was OK but the two girls Was just Showing off that is the stupidest thing I have heard Anyone Could be On the front page in a Comic Well anyway this is What girl's like. Theg like bad Stories good Stories, Stories about Scools, and Adventures, and they like boys in the story as well and they like Mixed Stories with a bit of everything in it. from

age 10.

LANGUAGE, RACISM AND ANTI-RACIST TEACHING

Marion Pencavel

When looking at how language can be racist and also how it can be used in anti-racist teaching, it is difficult to separate the issue from class. The use of British working-class dialects and accents is regarded as negatively as the use of non-European accents and languages. For this reason I will be looking at both these issues, though with particular emphasis on racism. Sexism in language is another area where there are overlaps, but as this issue is rather more distinct from race, and has been dealt with very well by Dale Spender[1], amongst others, it is not an area I am going to tackle in this article, although I would urge people not to think that it is any less important than the other two issues – racism and classism.

Up until fairly recently – to about the 1960s – there was never any doubt in the minds of most educationalists that one of the purposes of a 'good' education was to ensure that everyone spoke English with Received Pronunciation – no matter what their background. Any deviation from this was regarded as bad English and had to be corrected, both in speech and writing. It was also regarded as essential that anyone considering higher education should have at least 'O' level Latin, French and possibly another European language. To a certain extent these ideas have not changed very much; it is still regarded as important by most teachers including ourselves to ensure that all their pupils speak and write standard English, and although Latin is no longer essential, the upper classes still send their daughters to finishing schools to perfect their French, and being able to speak a modern European language still opens the doors to several high status professions.

There have been a few positive changes in attitudes to accents and dialects, however. It is now fairly common to hear regional accents on the radio and television – though not different dialects – and it is no longer essential to speak with R.P. in order to ensure a place at Oxbridge or in any other hallowed academic institution, nor to get a job within most professions. Poetry, plays and other works of literature are written in dialect – both UK English and others such as Jamaican English – and given due regard in their own right – within a certain section of the population at least. The ability to speak more than one language, however, is still not regarded very highly, especially if you happen to be fluent in a non-European language, or languages, as well as speaking English more or less fluently. There are many British people and people from overseas now settled permanently in Britain, who are bi-lingual or even ambi-lingual, yet because they speak English with a certain accent, or maybe have not yet learnt English if they have only recently arrived, are regarded as having 'no language' or being stupid and are encouraged to forget their own language(s) – and also to forget and reject their own culture – in favour of being totally immersed in English. Hazel Carby in her article *Schooling in Babylon*[2] looks at research and ideas in the 1960s which confirm the existence of this negative attitude.

If you look closely at the people this happens to, they fit into a certain category – those who have come from the 'underdeveloped' 'third world' countries. Those labels immediately make certain assumptions about the people. Likewise, if you look at those people who speak English with a low status accent or dialect, they also fit into a certain category – the urban or rural working class. With regard to bilinguals, think of the problems facing Asian teachers and pupils, compared to European teachers and pupils. French, German and Spanish teachers – often speaking English imperfectly and with a heavy accent – are welcomed into schools, either to teach their mother-tongue or other subjects. Pupils speaking those languages are not regarded as problems in class, because "they'll pick up English quickly" and their accents and attempts at speaking English are enjoyed. Asian teachers in particular have been discriminated against. White parents and teachers have complained that they cannot understand them, that this will hinder their children's educational development and that they should not be teaching white children anyway.[3] Asian pupils come up against similar reactions, and are regarded as being the cause of low achievement in a class or school, because "they take up so much of a teacher's time".

If an English speaking person has a strong Cockney, Irish or country accent, amongst others, they will often be thought of as having a low intelligence, until they can prove otherwise, while people speaking with a standard S.E. England accent are assumed to be well-educated and therefore intelligent – again possibly until they prove otherwise.

It is because of all these stereotyped images we have and use against certain people that these issues have been raised and must be dealt with.

Luckily, a lot of people are growing concerned about these racist and classist attitudes, and some teachers see that these attitudes are incompatible with child-centred education, now a generally accepted method of teaching in many primary schools. Most teachers would generally agree with Bullock's view that "The teacher should start where the child is and should accept the langue he (sic) brings to school." Also that "No child should be expected to cast off the language and culture of the home as he (sic) crosses the school threshold, nor to live and act as though school and home represent two totally separate and different cultures which have to be kept firmly apart." If we as teachers really believe in those statements, we need to rethink many of the ideas that we were brought up on, particularly if we were at college in the 60s and early 70s.

However, let me add at this point that what is *not* being advocated is the *teaching* of accents and dialects, nor the exclusion of teaching children to read and write standard English (if there is such a thing, which many linguists dispute). It is also important to remember the right of a child to have a 'private' language, that she/he can use with friends and the family, and not to force it to be used in class, if she/he doesn't want to do so. Mother tongue teaching is now recognised as being of educational as well as of social value and is dealt with elsewhere in this book. The use and acceptance of various dialects and accents, and a knowledge of both European and non-European languages are however crucial issues here. What we are saying is that teachers and other adults and pupils must value the language children use at home or in the playground, as being a part of that child and her/his family. Assumptions must not be made about that child (or adult) based solely on the sort of language she/he speaks, and teachers must not expect every child to talk the way she/he does (if that teacher happens to communicate and to explore new ideas. We are also saying that children need to be allowed to explore when certain types of language are appropriate, and when they are not. In fact, most children are experts already at changing from one way of speaking to another, whether that entails switching languages, dialects or just lessening a local accent, as well as at using familiar or more formal styles of speaking, just as most adults are. What they need is time to discuss this and to understand what they are doing, so they can make the same switches in writing, which is a more difficult skill, though again, one which many children pick up fairly instinctively, especially if they are already interested in language in general and in reading in particular.

The reasons for the switch in thinking over the last 20–30 years are based on teachers' knowledge of research by people such as Bernstein and Labov. Bernstein's work of the 1960s on elaborated and restricted codes in speech was very highly regarded in educational circles. Although a lot of his work has been mis-interpreted, and he himself has modified his theories in the light of newer research and much criticism, many teachers still agree with what they thought he originally said and use those ideas to form the basis of the language work they do in schools. The work of Labov and other socio-linguists has put another view to teachers, however, and because of this a more positive attitude to children's language is coming about. In practice, this has meant that teachers, instead of assuming that children who come to school speaking any form of 'non-standard' English are linguistically deficient, and need to have their speech 'improved', are more willing to accept the way a child speaks naturally, and will not inhibit her/him by continual correction, which causes far more damage than the possible lack of knowledge of standard English.

If a child is being made to feel a failure in some way by being continually corrected, not only will that child probably give up trying to communicate within the classroom, but will also be made to feel that there is something wrong with the way she/he and her/his family speak at home. This idea of failure is also communicated to other children, whose English is acceptable and thus not corrected, and so gives them the idea that they are superior in some way to the child who apparently needs so much correction. Thus are the seeds of class and race superiority sown, ready to be fuelled by any racist propaganda that is being put out by the media, the government, the school, or any of the innumerable places that consciously or unconsciously support the current ideology.

I will give one more example of the way different pieces of research have been used by teachers to change their ideas and practice. Bullock states that a "School Council project carried out tests which showed that (W.I.) dialect impeded the children's learning of English in the areas of oral comprehension, spoken intelligibility, reading, writing and spelling." The effect of other English dialects was often thought to be similar, though perhaps not to the same degree. However, since that time, more research has shown that this isn't the case. When a child is learning to read, and trying to make sense of a line of print, she/he will often miscue many of the words, yet will show that she/he has understood what has been printed, although interpreted it in a way that was meaningful to her/him. If a teacher continually corrects a child at this stage of learning, by asking the child to 'look at the ending of the word' etc. the child will feel that she/he is not able to read correctly, and will probably give up trying, as I have mentioned before. However, miscueing is just a normal learning process which all children go through in one form or another, not only in reading, but in speaking and writing as well.

Although language is often used subconsciously in a classist or racist way, there are more obvious ways that language can be racist. Racist name-calling is unfortunately a fairly common occurrence in schools and on the streets, and although most teachers recognise this as upsetting for children, only a few recognise how much more harmful it is than other types of name-calling based on other characteristics – names such as 'fatty' 'four-eyes' 'shorty' etc. Racist name-calling *must* be dealt with by teachers, not ignored. If we allow right-wing groups to chant political slogans, or allow scientists to put forward incorrect ideas 'proving' that blacks are inferior to whites, then we are legitimising what they are saying by our refusal to challenge them. Teachers who say to children complaining about racist name-calling, "ignore what they say, it's not worth making a fuss about, they don't mean anything by it", are doing the same thing in the eyes of their black pupils. If we didn't live in a racist society, maybe it wouldn't matter so much, but our society *is* racist, and gradually becoming more open about it, as the State (in the form of the government, the police, the law, etc.) obviously supports the perpetuation of a racist ideology. Taking that fact for granted then, why is it that racist abuse is so hurtful and damaging? As a white person, I find it difficult to answer that. Being called 'white honky' in a society where whites have the power is not the same as being called 'nig-nog' in the same society. The only way to find out how it really feels is by reference to contributions from black (or other ethnic or racial minority) people showing what it does to them. Ossie Davis in 1967 talked about how to him, the use of racist language was as vicious as a physical attack:

"Those words are attacks upon your physical and emotional well-being, your pulse rate is possibly higher, your breath quicker; there is perhaps a tremor along the nerves of your arms and legs; sweat begins in the palms of your hands, perhaps."

Since then, many more black people have articulated how it feels to be on the receiving end of racist abuse. (See, for example, the ALTARF Open Door film, *Racism – the Fourth R*) If you have a close enough relationship with a black pupil or adult, ask them how they feel. You'll find that most regard it as an attack on their whole being, or on their culture, or on all black people, or give one of many possible reactions. And if they trust you, most will say how much it hurts. A black teenage boy of my acquaintance, well aware of the racism in society and in his school, tries to avoid situations where name-calling and racist abuse might come up. He had problems with one member of the school basket-ball team, so rather than confront or try to ignore him, he left the team, although he loved playing. As the school is one where issues such as racism are not discussed, he didn't tell the teacher why he left. He is now probably regarded as unreliable, and will no doubt suffer in other ways in future because that sort of reputation is not so easily dismantled once stuck. His (white) friends from primary school also have little to do with him now – not because he or they have changed so much, but because they don't want to suffer taunts of 'nigger-lover' etc. that no doubt would be hurled at them when the teachers' backs are turned. Unless teachers are prepared to take up these issues, their pupils – black and white – will go on suffering. Until these issues are brought into the open, black children, especially of secondary age, will 'gang' together – not to cause trouble, but to avoid the hurt that may come when associating with their white peers. Apart from being seen as threatening by some adults, this will lessen the range of friends both black and white children may have.

If children are being hurt in our schools, how can they be in a fit state to learn? If children are hurting others, how can they be in the right frame of mind to be able to learn? Rosa Guy, the black American author, said in a talk to a group of teachers, "Hatred destroys the self before it destroys the other."

Thus a child with racist ideas, who is trying to hurt others by expressing those ideas, will end up suffering more in the long term than those she/he is abusing. So not only is racial abuse harmful to those at the receiving end, it is also harmful to the perpetrator.

Apart from all the moral reasons for getting rid of racist name-calling, there are sound educational ones as well. It is well-known that people learn best when they are happy, secure, and feel free to make mistakes. Emotional upsets are bound to affect the learning of both instigator and sufferer. That is why we must also be aware of all the negative connotations around the word 'black' and all the positive ones around the word 'white'. Although many people feel that this is rather silly and taking things too far, the use of such words and phrases as 'blackmail', 'black-list', 'a black book', 'black-leg' etc. do reinforce the racism in our society, even though it may be subconscious. Yuri Yevtushenko, the Russian poet, on hearing of the assassination of Martin Luther King, wrote:

His skin was black
but with the purest soul,
white as the snow . . .

Why should Martin Luther King have to be given a *white* soul in order to praise him? What is wrong with a *black* soul – except the connotation that surrounds that phrase?

Institutional language can also be racist and classist. One of the reasons for making sure that pupils learn to speak and write standard English when they need to, is in order for them to be able to cope with the language that is used within the various institutions they will come across – the tax office, the social security, courts, arranging hire-purchase etc. It is also important that they understand why this language is the way it is, so they are not intimidated by it, but are able to fight against the unnecessary use of such language. Why should certain groups of people be able to lay down how others should write in certain circumstances? Why should we have to put up with convoluted, archaic forms of English jargon in order to provide business for lawyers etc, and to perpetuate the mystique of such professions – and their fees? Why should people who can't read English at the level required by official forms be made to suffer humiliation at having to ask, inconvenience at having to wait or find someone to help, and often poverty because an incorrectly filled-in form means that they can't get money that is owed to them?

Why also should people not brought up to speak standard English be penalised for not understanding the conventions that go with the use of that language? In every society, there are polite and impolite ways of speaking, listening, agreeing and disagreeing. A child who looks away and says nothing when being told off by a teacher may well be behaving perfectly by her/his own standards. If the teacher doesn't understand this, that child is labelled insolent or dumb, and treated in future accordingly. These are the sorts of issues teachers must raise with their pupils, or allow their pupils to raise with them, for their own sakes and for the sake of others who may come into contact with them in the future.

To finish this article, I would like to re-assure parents, pupils and teachers that basing teaching about language on ideas like these does not lead to a 'fall in standards'. Although traditional methods are/were not without their succcesses (mainly for the middle and upper classes, however) our society has changed over the last few decades, and will continue to change. Education must change with it, and the consciousness that is developing among some people that life could be better for everyone, not just the 'lucky' few, and that Victorian values are not what we want to see being put into practice, must be built on. This means that education has to be political – not putting forward the doctrines of any particular party, but enabling future generations to be capable of articulate criticism of wrongs they see around them.

We also want to ensure that children – and adults – are committed to fighting for a more just society – we don't want pupils using their information and skills to perpetuate and develop an *unjust* one. It is unfortunately possible for well-educated people to be racist – it is not just ignorance that causes racism – and when these people are in positions of power, as many of them are today, it needs a well-informed, articulate, politicised body of people at grassroots level to fight against them.

A thorough understanding of language will help in that fight. People need to be able to look at language from the outside, objectively, and see how it can be manipulated, as well as how it has developed and is continually developing, rather than merely to accept it as it is and assume it is just natural, always the same, and unable to be changed. This sort of knowledge, together with the more traditional knowledge of language skills, will help in the fight against racism, and also help pupils to succeed in the school system as it is at present – to pass exams and to go on to further and higher education if they so wish. The skills of discussion, debate, and listening to others are very important educational lessons to learn, as Bullock pointed out in 1975. Unfortunately, these skills are still greatly undervalued, yet they are crucial if we and our pupils or children are to be able to involve ourselves in the fight for a more just society.

Education, including learning skills such as reading and writing, is a political issue. Teachers and parents ignore that dimension at their peril.

The final section of this article, in conjunction with the chapter on 'Mother Tongue', looks at practical ways in which teachers can put these ideas into practice. Racism as an issue does not appear overtly except in the section 'The printed word'. However, that doesn't mean that it has been ignored. If teachers take on any of these ideas, they will be providing a forum for debate, where all sorts of issues will be raised, and will be providing the right sort of atmosphere for pupils to feel free to discuss very personal issues, including racism, sexism and classism.

These ideas are also based on the premise that teachers and schools are using teaching methods based on generally accepted good primary practice, as has been mentioned before – child-centred, collaborative learning, a classroom atmosphere conducive to the free exchange of ideas between pupil and pupil, and pupils and teachers, and a full involvement of the school with the local community. Unless these things are accepted by the school, then many of the suggested activities will be impossible or may even have the opposite effect to that intended. Language is a very personal, sensitive area of the curriculum, and some of the ideas that follow should just be used as and when a suitable moment appears, especially with very young children. Teachers will obviously have to adapt and expand the suggestions to fit their particular knowledge and circumstances.

1 Dale Spender *Man Made Language*
2 Hazel Carby *Schooling in Babylon* in *The Empire Strikes Back* Centre for Contemporary Cultural Studies, Hutchinson University Library 1982
3 Errol Lawrence in *Just Plain Common Sense* in *The Empire Strikes Back* op cit

VISUAL IMPACT

Suggestions:

* Notices — welcoming parents in different languages (see LMS poster and Bedford stuff)
  — directions in appropriate languages
* Labels in different languages
* Children's work in different languages, dialects or styles in prominent positions
* Names for numbers and colours in different languages and scripts (and in transliteration)
* Alphabet charts

→

Ways of using the suggestions:

Oral:
* Discussions on each visual as it goes up
* Pupils talking about own writing (bilingual pupils translating or bidialectal explaining)
* Pupils teaching each other greetings, numbers, letters, etc., in different languages & dialects
* Pupils learning how and when to write different styles, dialects

COMMUNITY LINKS

Suggestions:

Using pupils, parents, teachers and others as a resource:
* Making books
* Translating
* Visits to local & 'distant' environment (incl. shops)
* Dance and Drama
* Telling stories and putting on to tapes

→

Ways of using the suggestions:

Oral / Written:

Vast possibilities — please see resource list

SIGNS, SYMBOLS AND PICTURES

Suggestions:

* Picture languages
* Other systems of communication, e.g. notes, Braille, semaphore, hieroglyphics, cherokee, etc.
* Traffic and other public signs in Britain and abroad

→

Ways of using the suggestions:

Oral:

* Discussions about different issues relating to suggestions, e.g. why are certain pictures/signs etc. used?
* Where will you find them?
* How do you know?
* Who will use them?

Written:

* Write letters in different systems
* Make up own versions
* See if your friend can read your message

See resource list for more details/ideas

THE PRINTED WORD

Suggestions:

* Remove the worst out-dated, racist books in the school
* Find as many good, positive books as possible to replace them
* Look at comic books and newspapers from different backgrounds, especially in different languages

→

Ways of using the suggestions:

Oral:

* Discussion of why books have been removed
* Discuss racist, sexist, classist bias
* Discussion of why other books are better
* Raising pupil's level of critical awareness
* Using taped dialogues or stories — elicit background of speaker and meaning of story, if in another language etc.

Written:

* Making own newspaper, comic, books using languages, dialects in the school
* Making examples of good, non-racist, non-sexist books (and publishing them!)
* Make books bi- or ambi-lingual where possible

THE SPOKEN WORD

Suggestions:

* Listen to different dialects, accents, languages on tape and around school, on radio, TV, etc.
* Set up a listening corner

→

Ways of using the suggestions:

Oral:

* Drama, using different accents, dialects, languages to allow children to explore when it is appropriate to use specific accents, etc.
* Discussion on styles of speech, how languages evolve and are constantly changing
* Making own tapes

Written:

* Putting the spoken word into print — using the appropriate styles
* Reading the written representation of spoken word

GAMES, STORIES, SONGS & RHYMES

Suggestions:

* Collect these from different cultures and in different languages
* Get pupils to teach these to others – and enjoy them!
* Build up own tape/cassette library of above in different languages

→

Ways of using the suggestions:

Oral:

* Comparing across cultures/languages, etc.
* Origins of these (discuss)
* Learning simple counting rhymes etc., in another language
* Making up own games, etc.

Written:

* Writing instructions for games (bilingual if possible)
* Writing own stories, songs, rhymes in different dialects and languages

CURRICULUM AREAS

Some of these ideas are suitable for starting projects e.g. the history of writing or numbers, while others will fit better into an on-going project e.g. information about names from the different cultures will fit into a project on the local area.

Suggestions:

* Names and Naming systems
* Changing names
* History of writing and number systems
* Topic work on:
  - environmental studies
  - food
  - ourselves/families
  - communications, etc.

→

Ways of using the suggestions:

Oral / Written:
Vast possibilities — please see resource list

MOTHER TONGUE

Doreen Medcraft

While seldom denying the importance of mother tongue maintenance at home, many teachers are ambivalent about the use of children's first languages in schools. Their concern is usually underlain by fears of segregation and marginality for the children involved, and about the wider political implications of mother tongue teaching. Yet other, less sympathetic, teachers query the whole educational basis of first language maintenance in school, and believe this to be a concern of the home alone. In this article I would like to argue the case for mother tongue maintenance within the primary classroom, and seek to allay the fears of teachers who believe the issue to be divisive or politically biased. Although this article deals with languages, the arguments put forward equally apply to dialects. And it must be remembered that Britain is not the only country to have a variety of regional accents and dialects. Indeed, many of the children for whom English is a second language, speak a regional variation of their first language. This may present a number of problems for the child, not least of which is the recognition of that dialect, and the ability to switch to a standard form without losing her/his own regional variety.

The myth of bilingualism as a handicap still lingers in Britain[1]. While the rich send their children to French Finishing schools, the poor are informed through social attitudes, the media and street racism that their first language or dialect is invalid and useless. Small wonder that many parents discourage their children from speaking the first language at school; tragically this can extend to the home also. In the past non-standard English dialects have been rejected as 'bad' or ungrammatical. These days, but only since the seventies, regional accents are considered 'acceptable' by the media. Dialects do not fare so well, featuring only in occasional drama productions. The low status of particular regional variations reflects class and race divisions. Geordie and Cockney suffer for their working class roots while Jamaican English has the double handicap of both class and race prejudice. (See Language, Racism and Anti-Racist Teaching article in this book.)

Children who speak another language at home are trapped in a potentially damaging situation. They are made to feel that in order to identify with the majority culture and to succeed, they must reject the language and culture of home. Inevitably, those children fail, due in large measure to the inherent racism which is so much a part of the British cultural heritage. Until fairly recently, it was assumed that the lack of success at school of children who spoke another language at home was a direct cause and effect. During the fifties and sixties 'Mother tongue interference' was cited as the major cause of school underachievement. The theory that once the family had abandoned their distinctive culture and language, they would somehow miraculously be 'assimilated' still has echoes in schools today. The onus was always on the minority group to give way; had they all done so, the racism within our post-Colonial society would never have allowed 'assimilation'; this fact is conveniently ignored. Today, research shows us beyond any doubt, that the underachievement of minority group children is caused not by their culture and language/dialect, but by attempts to eradicate these. Bilingualism, as the rich have always known but never extrapolated to Africa or Asia, can be a positive force in the child's development when the first language is given status and promoted.

It is a mark of our double standards that Europeans

learning English are seldom considered to have any difficulties or problems. In fact their success is widely acknowledged in the schools, and their first language, especially should it be French or German, given prominence and status. Southern Europeans fare less well but still have their languages recognised as valid. Asians and Africans however, often suffer the humiliation of having their mother tongue ignored, confused with other languages or rejected outright. Look at the number of times one 'Chinese' child is assumed to be able to translate for any other far Eastern newcomer. How many teachers know which of their Chinese pupils speak Cantonese, Hakka, Wu or Vietnamese? How many assume Sylheti speakers to be as competent at learning English as a new Greek speaker? How many confuse Urdu with Gujerati, or Bengali with Punjabi? African children however, suffer the greatest rejection when they discover teachers have not even heard of their languages. The number of times 'African' or 'Nigerian' is given as a child's first language in ILEA's two yearly Language Surveys, has only decreased slightly in the last decade.

Four major research projects demonstrate the positive effects of mother tongue maintenance in schools. The Manitoba Francophone Study (1975)[2] showed that children receiving 80% of their education through the medium of French, and only 20% through English, did just as well in English as children receiving 80% in English and only 20% in French. Not only did they achieve as well in English, but this group also improved much more rapidly than the second group in French.

An American Indian Study, Rock Point Navajo Study (1971-1976)[2] used Navajo as the main means of communication. English reading was delayed until Navajo reading skills were well established. By these means, children who had previously been two years behind U.S. norms in English reading (in spite of intensive compensatory and ESL programmes) ended the project slightly above the standard U.S. Grade norms in reading in English – and all this despite considerably less use of the second language in school.

The Sodertalje Programme for Finnish speaking children in Sweden[3] produced similar results to the Navajo Study. The Finnish children were underachieving in both Finnish and Swedish when the study began. Again the medium of instruction was the mother tongue and again by top Junior age the children were performing at the same level as that of native Swedish speakers in Finland.

The Alberta Government funded a Ukrainian-English Bilingual Programme in the early seventies,[2] and this is still continuing into the eighties. By top Junior age, the children receiving 50% of their total education in Ukrainian were actually ahead of their monolingual peers in English reading comprehension skills, and obviously their first language had benefited considerably.

These are just four projects out of many initiatives throughout the world; but their findings demonstrate the correlation between maintenance of the first language in school and educational achievement. Moreover, the children studied also increased in confidence and self-esteem. The promotion of the first language had no detrimental effects on the second, in fact children became more proficient in both languages. So instead of discarding the child's abilities in the mother tongue, we can build on them to ensure continuity of learning and deeper understanding. That the child will learn English is inevitable in an English speaking environment; she/he is exposed to the second language through a variety of media. TV, radio, records, English speaking peers, teachers, community and all the structured ESL provision ensure that the second language is constantly practised, used and improved. Nevertheless it is the first language which is vital in securing early linguistic concepts: the development of these concepts is central to the child's overall intellectual and educational progress. As these concepts are acquired naturally in the first language, it is essential that the quality of speech in that language is as rich as possible. Once linguistic concepts are established in the first tongue, they may easily be transferred to the second language. Given the importance of this early development, the potentially disastrous effects of parents using inadequate or broken English in preference to their mother tongue become apparent. Gordon Wells 'Bristol Project'[4] demonstrated how vital is the quality of parent-child discourse, and how early linguistic development is positively correlated with the level of reading skills acquired in school. Parents who are 'persuaded' to use English in the home, or to curtail the use of mother tongue, reduce the quality of parent-child dialogue. This slows down the development of linguistic concepts and reduces the chance of the child achieving well in either language. On the other hand, parents who use the first language to full advantage at home give the child the necessary linguistic concepts which may later be transferred quite easily to English.

In considering political implications of mother tongue maintenance, it is important to bear in mind the positive linguistic, social and educational advantages outlined above. Certainly the EEC Directive on Mother Tongue Teaching has the underlying purpose of keeping a floating European population of migrants, already schooled in their first language and home culture, ready to be expelled from a country if economic circumstances demand. Nevertheless we cannot deny children a right to the advantages of bilingualism with all that this implies for self-confidence, esteem, and overall academic and intellectual development, simply because the motives and sincerity of the EEC are suspect. Nor, I believe, should we listen to critics who see mother tongue maintenance as another form of state social control, without weighing the positive factors very carefully. Of course, if the first language is taught solely to act as a control on the parents, then it is bound to fail, and deserves to be exposed for the political manoeuvring that it is; but if first language teaching is integral to the curriculum, so that it is seen to be an essential part of that curriculum, then the assimilationist/social control theory no longer applies. Communication will be two-way. Parents will be able to come to school freely to discuss with teachers; they will have an important role to play as the school seeks further ways of working with, through and for the local community. It is up to us to see that mother tongue is never used to bolster an authoritarian school system, where it is merely the vehicle to transmit rules and regulations.

I believe that the worry of segregation or marginalisation of children being taught in their first language can be overcome by organising the learning in new ways. It means careful time-tabling to avoid withdrawal if at all possible. Ideally withdrawal should only occur when there is a general distribution of groups around the school. If children leave the class at the same time every day, then not only do they run the risk of missing out on whole areas of the curriculum, but more important, they become 'different' from their peers. A school interested in developing mother tongue teaching must consider these essential organisational strategies as a whole: it may be that team teaching answers the problem best in certain schools; possibly there could be work across class divisions or age groups. Best of all is mother tongue teaching within the classroom – this, more than any rhetoric will show the school's commitment and it avoids possible stigmatisation. In general, Infant and Junior schools are very flexible, and it does not seem an insurmountable task to develop mother tongue group work so that it is part of the curriculum, linking very clearly with all other school activities.

Most of us are, unfortunately, monolingual speakers

of English. As such we are in a world minority; most people in India speak Hindi as well as their own first language, and many know English. In Uganda everyone is bilingual; some know four or five different languages and switch from one to another with ease. Many Vietnamese children speak Cantonese and Vietnamese. And all East Africans know Swahili as well as their mother tongue. The dominance of English in geographically scattered parts of the world reflects the colonial history of the old 'British Empire'. It also acts as an indicator of the status conferred on different languages and cultures by the early colonialists. African cultures were systematically down graded and humiliated or patronised. Racist theories were evolved to justify the appalling conditions of slavery, by permanently discriminating on grounds of colour and alleged genetic inferiority. Asian cultures did not suffer to the same extent, but were nevertheless accorded much lower status than white British culture. A hierarchy of languages matched a hierarchy of peoples and cultures, with English at the apex, grading down through European languages and Asian tongues to everything black and African at the bottom. This is not just a relic, an embarrassing historical fact – the racist beliefs engendered by slavery and the Empire still live in the cultural repertoire of present day Britain. It is vital that we do all we can to confront racism in schools, to substitute facts for prejudice about cultures and languages other than our own, and to build a curriculum suitable to the needs of all children. I believe mother tongue maintenance is something we can all attempt, even if we are monolingual ourselves. Not all schools will be able to initiate a full first language teaching programme, but most can help to promote an awareness of, and an interest in, children's home languages, and to work towards supporting and maintaining the mother tongues of children in their schools.

The reasons for supporting children's first languages

are not only educational. In fact the most important follows from the historical setting above; namely, that it gives validity to the child's culture. Anything that promotes respect from the majority group will enhance the minority child's confidence and self-esteem, and give her/him pride in her/his abilities. The fact that maintenance of the mother tongue in school has a beneficial effect on the development of English, is an added bonus. Schools committed to supporting mother tongue often find parents developing an interest in school activities; parents are no longer cut off from their children by another language which they can't understand.[5] Children can have a fuller relationship with their parents and the community. And, as previously outlined, the quality of parent-child interaction is enhanced by using the first language – this will further the child's academic, social and intellectual progress.

How can mother tongue be maintained then? There are many simple things a school can do to increase the use of a child's first language. These come under seven main headings: (see diagram pp.141–144)

1. Visual Impact
2. Community Links
3. Signs, Symbols, Pictures
4. Printed Word
5. Spoken Word
6. Games, Stories, Songs, Rhymes
7. Curricula Areas

1. Visual Impact

There must be visual evidence that the school is aware of its pupils languages. 'Welcome' notices and posters should be displayed in the relevant scripts. The 'LMS' Welcome Poster has most languages and spaces for any others necessary. Classwork and displays can easily include mother tongue work or bilingual writing. Many class themes and topics may be pursued in the child's first language. Children enjoy working with bilingual friends on comparisons across languages e.g. Numbers 1–10 in all languages/dialects spoken in the school or Family Words (Mum, Dad, etc.) across all thc languages. Labels and directions around the school could be made for the appropriate languages. Alphabet charts in many of the most widely spoken languages are available (see resources list).

2. Community Links

Local community links are easier to establish once the school makes a commitment to mother tongue maintenance. Everyone may be looked upon as a resource; parents, teachers, pupils, older brothers and sisters – they may all be encouraged to come into the school to tell stories, translate writing and books, record cassette tapes or make books. Helping with a special project is obviously valuable, but so too is coming in on a more regular basis, even if the activity seems mundane. AEIs often run Mother Tongue and ESL classes for adults. If these are in your school building make contact, and try some joint projects. Community Schools are also interested in becoming more involved with LEA schools – they frequently feel isolated from the British educational system, and welcome liaison. It is often possible to enlarge resources and make more personal contacts through forging links with Community Schools. Of course, contact with other Primary schools in the area can provide much stimulus and reveal expertise which joint visits may draw upon.

3. Signs, Symbols, Pictures

Once children become interested in their own and other languages, they like to find out about different systems of communication, e.g. codes, Braille, Semaphore, heiroglyphs, picture languages and ideographs. Signs in other places are also interesting to investigate e.g. road signs, street/shop signs – in English and other languages.

The World in a City

CRE/Learning Materials Service, ILEA

4. *Printed Word*

The library and classrooms should ideally have a good selection of mother tongue and bilingual books. Check suitable books (those with no text or a limited amount) in order to write in a translation or your own script in appropriate languages. (See resources list for suggestions.) Throw out the worst old-fashioned, racist books. Do this as a staff; discuss the reasons. Talk about sexist books too. Try to leave a few bad books depicting a certain country and language to:

(a) contrast with positive books on the same area
(b) use for discussion with older classes/new staff.

Build up a collection of good, positive books – bilingual, mother tongue and English.

ILEA teachers should use CLRS who have a collection of books in mother tongue. The more teachers who request books, the more pressure will be applied to CLRS to increase their stock.

Use the local libraries too. They are able to obtain reasonable selections of both mother tongue and bilingual books. Do ask, even if you cannot see any – extra pressure on the Central Libraries can be most productive. Many children's librarians are very keen to know what sort of books children want, and in which languages; they will often buy specific titles too.

Wherever possible school documents, forms, letters, brochures, etc. should be available in the languages appropriate to the school. Many standard LEA forms are obtainable in a variety of languages.

5. *Spoken Word*

A good collection of cassette tapes in mother tongue is invaluable. Stories, rhymes and songs may be contributed by parents and pupils. Every classroom should have a listening corner, where children can hear tapes in their first language while reading the script from bilingual or mother tongue books. This helps to establish literacy. Make use of mother tongue when the whole school is present too; plays and drama, assemblies and celebrations. Do not exclude newly arrived children with little English: the fluent bilinguals can help them to take an active part from the start.

Language in the playground and around the school is most important; the employment of bilingual ancillaries and teachers should be one of our priorities.

6. *Games, Stories, Songs and Rhymes*

Ideally the school should have a comprehensive selection of these from different cultures and languages. A Cassette tape library could be built up. Children who know a game, story, song or rhyme could teach it to the other children and teachers. Many themes in traditional stories, games and songs cross national boundaries – comparisons lead to interesting discussions about origins etc.

7. *Curricula Areas*

This has almost endless possibilities. Themes and topics within the school will all benefit from extension into other languages and cultures, e.g. environmental studies, food, ourselves, families communication, animals, water, homes, etc.

Some ideas are suitable for starting projects e.g. writing systems, Naming systems, A History of Numbers, etc.

Finally, consider two issues – Staffing and School Policy. None of the above suggestions will be totally effective without school policy on mother tongue (linked with the Anti-Racist Policy) and the full commitment of head and staff to the employment of bilingual class teachers, ancillaries and mother tongue specialists.

BIBLIOGRAPHY

1. *Bilingualism in Education* – John Wright.
2. *Mother Tongue Maintenance for Minority Language Children* – Jim Cummins, 1982.
3. *Sodertalje Programme for Finnish speaking Immigrant Children in Sweden* – Skutnabb - Kangas and Toukomaa, 1976.
4. *The Bristol Project* – Gorden Wells, University of Bristol School of Education.
5. Amrit Wilson – *Finding a Voice* – Virago, 1980.
6. *1981 & 83 Language Census* – ILEA Research and Statistics, County Hall, London SE1.

RESOURCES

1. *'From Home to School'* booklets for parents in English, Punjabi and Urdu. Coventry Community Education Project, Coventry Education Office, Coventry.
2. *Posters for Celebrations* in Urdu, Bengali, Hindi, Punjabi, Gujerati, Chinese and Italian. M.E.R.C., Tennyson Road Primary School, Tennyson Road, Luton LU1 3RS. (Luton 26880)
3. Learning Materials Service, ILEA, Highbury Station Road, London N1 1SB. (01-226 9143) They publish:
   (a) *Welcome Poster* (in 29 languages)
   (b) *The first Few Weeks* – phrase books in Chinese, Gujerati, Punjabi and Urdu.
   (c) *The World in a City* – 40 bilingual cards for top Juniors or Secondary – 8 languages available.
   (d) *Maps / Photos from Bangladesh.*
4. *Alphabet Charts* – in Urdu, Gujerati, Hindi and Bengali from Soma Bookshop, 38 Kennington Lane, London SE11 4LS. (01-735 2101)
5. *The Languages Book – for top Junior/Secondary.* Available from The English Centre, Sutherland Street, London SW1. (ILEA)
6. Health Education Council. *Posters in various languages.* Suitable for older children and parents.
7. ILEA Interpreters/Translators. Team Organiser: Mr Theodosiou, Room 435A, County Hall, London SE1. (01-633 1448)
   Languages include: Bengali, Cantonese, Greek, Turkish, Gujerati, Hindi, Punjabi, Urdu, Spanish, Arabic and Vietnamese.
8. Library Loans: ILEA's Central Library Resources Service, CLRS, Loans Division, 275 Kennington Lane, London SE11 5QZ. (633 5982) for ILEA teachers – a growing collection in most languages.

continued

9. Books:
   (a) *'City Kids'* Series (Nelson) available in Turkish, Greek, Italian, English and no text.
   (b) *'Terraced House'* Books (Methuen) available with stick-on scripts in Bengali.
   (c) *'Instant Readers'* (Methuen) You can add your own translation to make books bilingual.
   (d) Books with no text or only a very limited one, lend themselves to addition of another script/translation, e.g. *The Trunk* and *Cat on the Mat* – B. Wildsmith (O.U.P.). *Do You Want to be my Friend?* – E. Carle, Picture Puffins. *Look Again* – Hamish Hamilton. *Sunshine* and *Moonlight* – Kestrel/Picture Puffins. *Changes, Changes* – Bodley Head.
   (e) *Folktales from Australia's Children of the World* – Ure Smith. Stories in English and language of origin, available widely in Forbuoys, etc.
   (f) *Indian languages* – A very large collection of books available from Soma Bookshop, 38 Kennington Lane, SE11. (01-735 2101) Many others in bookshops on list.
   (g) *Chinese language & bilingual Chinese/English books.* Very good selection at Guangwa Co., 7-9 Newport Place, London WC2. (01-437 3737)
   (h) *Turkish, Greek, Arabic and European language books.*

10. *'Learn Your Language'* Series of Bengali booklets and primers for children. Available from Mrs. Buksh, 38 Umfreville Road, London N4.

AN INTERVIEW WITH WENDY

Martin Francis and Wendy Scott

This is an interterview with Wendy, an 11 year old, recorded just after she had transferred from primary to secondary school.

I'd like to hear about some of the things you have already done at your secondary school to try to change things or problems that you've had.

Well the three girls who used to come to this primary school tried to start a girls group at Holland Park so we could discuss our problems or any racist names or anything that we wanted to talk about that was bothering us and we would take it to our head of year or our year council (counsel?). So we got together with Lesley our Sports teacher and we had a talk about what we'd like to do and things we'd like to talk about and she said that instead of just doing it up in assembly and talking about it we could make a leaflet and we didn't get round to doing that after about three weeks because we didn't have much time and so eventually we did get to do one and when the leaflets have been passed out we'll start a girls group.

What sort of things do you want to talk about?

The girls who are mostly coming are black, that's in our class anyway, and so we'll talk about racism and any racism things we've had and anything we think we could do good in Holland Park about racism and what could be done about it.

From your first six weeks at Holland Park do you think there are teachers there who will take up what you say and will do something about it?

Well I think so. There are a couple of teachers who would be interested. Some of them might not – some of them might – I don't know really – 'cause I think most of them would be . . .

How many teachers know about what you're doing?

Only two teachers because they're the only ones we've been talking to about it but when the leaflet goes out I expect all the teachers will know and then we'll get more people who'd like to take part and the teachers will be more interested about things we're going to do.

Having just left this Primary school and gone to Secondary school is there a difference in the way teachers deal with racist incidents – name calling and so on?

Well in this school (the primary) if you did used to be called a name some teachers might say 'Go away', 'Ignore them' or things like that or nothing was done about it or tell them off and that was it and they kept on doing it because they kept on doing it because they thought nothing was going to be done about it so that was it. But in Holland Park if you're called a racist name or anything the child or children who did it would get in real serious trouble because they don't like it because in big writing on one side of the school they've got: 'Holland Park is an international school' so I think they'll deal with it and the person would deal with them severely.

Can you tell us about an incident that happened at this school with you, Monique and Mandy when you were called a name and what you did about it?

Well we were in the playground just walking about minding our own business and this boy had an argument with a black boy and he started coming up to us and

and calling *us* names so we told him to go away and he wouldn't go away so we went up to the teacher and this teacher didn't do anything about it and just told us to ignore him, leave him alone and just called him up and said, 'Jason stop it' and that's it – she didn't do nothing else so we kept on going up to the teacher and still nothing was done about it so when we got in the classroom we all decided that what we were going to do was do no work until something satisfactory was done about racism. So then we didn't do any work and our teacher came up and he asked us why we weren't doing any work. We told him why and he said it was good that we tried to organise things about racism, do something about it and let teachers know what is happening.

When you were in this school we used to have discussions about racism, about sexism, about things that used to be in the news – do you still have discussions about things like that now at Holland Park?

No not yet, but the Girls Group we're setting up that's what we hope to talk about.

Do you think that teachers should set those sorts of things up or are you quite happy that it should be pupils themselves doing that and you don't want interference from teachers?

Well I think teachers should give a hand in it but also again I think that kids should try to do it themselves. So teachers can find out what they can do and use their imagination about things and how they can think of things to do. I think that it would be quite good if the teachers let the kids set up their own group and things like that.

When you had a Girls' Group at this school, was everybody in favour of it or did you find you had some problems getting started or continuing it?

Well we did start it and it was alright but when we used to be inside, third and fourth year kids used to keep running in and out and we used to keep shouting at them, 'Get out' and the dinner lady used to come in and tell *us* off for shouting and everything and tell the person off and we all used to get thrown out and I thought that wasn't fair because it wasn't us. She knew we were in there and each time she used to throw us out and I don't know why. We would have it in the Library and she didn't like us in there so we moved out and went in the Resource Area, she didn't like us in there so we moved in our own class and other dinner ladies used to send us out because they didn't like us in there – so in the end we never used to have it – we only used to have it when our teacher gave us our own free time and that was about it – that was the only time we had a chance to talk about it.

I remember something – not a racist incident. Remember when one of the boys insulted one of the girls in the class? Can you remember what you as the girls did about it?

Well, we did try and get Vincent to apologise but he wouldn't apologise so then we all decided that we wouldn't talk to the boys because of what Vincent had done and he just wouldn't apologise so we all had a talk to the boys telling them what they were doing had hurt us and that and they said that we used to hurt them by saying things about them when we didn't. They just wanted to say something to get their own back on us. We tried as much as possible to make him apologise and then finally he did apologise.

How did you finally get him to apologise? He came in on his own didn't he? How did he react to all the girls sitting there telling him what was wrong with the way he behaved.

Well at first he kept denying it and he wouldn't say

anything and then we said, 'Vincent you better apologise or this thing is going to go on for ages' – he still said he wasn't going to apologise so then we goes, 'Vincent, you hurt her and if you keep saying no you're not going to do anything about it, things are just going to get worse'. So in the end he just apologised.

How important was the teacher in that? In setting it up so that you had a separate Girls Group for him to go in and talk to? Would you have been able to do it without the teacher helping?

I think we needed the teacher in the fact that he gave us the permission to stay in and if we didn't have that permission we couldn't have done it, we couldn't have set it all up. So with the teacher we did get a few things to help – permission to stay in and time to discuss it. The teacher did give a good hand in it.

Can you tell us about the book review you and Mandy did? What do you think about books in school?

Well I think there isn't enough black books in school. They've got Peter and Jane and they're white and they haven't got any books for black kids and if they have they're just silly books – they're not sensible. So what we tried to do (which we never finished) we made up our own book after a programme about people getting jobs and racism. We did a book about jobs and drew pictures and we talked about why black people hadn't been getting jobs. Was it because of their colour or is it just because they're not qualified and we got to the decision that it was because of their colour. So what we did was we got together, we had a discussion before we started making the book, and we just started writing it down and drawing pictures about it. Two people from a black group who used to help people with housing and that came along and we had a discussion with all the kids and then about black children being called racist names and why black people aren't getting jobs, and if there's houses why only white people get moved in and things like that and we talked about it for some time.

What do you think about people like that coming into schools? Would you like those same people, because they work in Shepherds Bush, come to speak at Holland Park about what they do?

I think it would be good for people to come in and talk about it and let everyone know that it doesn't matter what colour you are – we're all humans.

What do you think about there being more black teachers?

There was a black teacher at school. The head master there was ill so as he was the deputy head he took the job while the head was away. (When the headship job eventually came up) he went for the job and didn't get it. We all talked about that and why he didn't get the job. We thought it was because he was black because the person who did get it was white.

What did the black and white kids in the discussion say about having a black head master? What did they think about black teachers?

Most of them said that they'd like a black teacher because they're more strict and they're hard. If you're in trouble most teachers are soft softies.

How do you think a black teacher would take up racist remarks? Do you think they would take them up differently from a white teacher?

Yes, because he's the same colour, he'd know what to expect, he'd have more feelings than the white teacher he (the white teacher) wouldn't have been called the name and wouldn't know how we feel.

Do you think it is possible for a white teacher to under-

stand at all what it is like to be black?

Not all of them. Just one or two, maybe – but not all of them.

How do you think that could be changed?

By more teachers having a lot more black kids in their class where they can find out the feeling of the class if they've been called any racist names.

Can you tell people about when we went to talk to a group of teachers about how they could change?

Well we said that they could have more groups, and more discussion with the children to find out more about the problems that they had, and how teachers could help us with the things we wanted to do, say if we were getting too easy homework they could discuss with us if we wanted harder – or if it was too hard and we wanted easier.

When me and six of you were sitting up there do you think they were taking notice of what we were saying?

At first we were all nervous, even the adults, and then when we started to talk a lot I think they were interested in what we were saying.

How do you think teachers react to children telling them how they should teach?

Some of them might not like it, because they should know, they went to train – but really they don't know the children's feelings, so that they don't understand how *we* feel.

So do you think there should be more places where children can go and tell teachers what they think about what is going on inside schools?

There should be more places, and time, so children can go to teachers and tell them if they think something is bothering them and nothing is being done about it.

What do you think about the way you've been encouraged to speak up for yourself and do you think that gets you into trouble sometimes?

I don't think it gets us into trouble because if you don't speak up for yourself, the teachers is going to think you did do it, because you're not speaking up for yourself – so you must have done it. But if you do speak up for yourself they will start to listen to your side of the story. You're not letting the other person, who you got into trouble with, talk for you – giving their side of the story and you not giving yours.

If we're doing all this inside the school, you know, talking about racism, telling children that racism harms people, about the history of racism, about what happened in Germany to the Jews and so on, does that still make sense if outside the school there are still problems with racism with say, how the police behave or remember when you told me about the Nationality Act? Do you think it's worth doing if all those things don't change? Or do you think we have to change those things as well?

I think it has to start in the school first because when you go from primary to secondary that's where it gets worse, getting called racist names and things like that. I think if it starts in the school first it will get better because (otherwise) the children who are in secondary school, they'll grow up to adults like the National Front are now. If they know what's happening when they're in schools there's a better chance of it getting better outside.

TALKING ABOUT RACE – PRIMARY AND SECONDARY SCHOOL STUDENTS MAKE LINKS

Introduction – *Sue Birchall*
Article – *Mary Bull & Karen Gibson*

Introduction

The following article sets out how a group of sixth form students came to meet younger children to talk about their experiences of racism. The meetings were initiated by the sixth formers who were anxious to alert the younger children to institutional racism and to help them develop the confidence to cope with and perhaps challenge this.

In their own school the sixth formers had begun to articulate memories from their schooling which they interpreted as institutionalised racism. The girls were a mixed group with backgrounds in Africa, Europe, Asia and the Caribbean. The assumptions of teachers that Black girls are good at sport, that bilingual children cannot cope with English 'O' levels, the understanding that a banding system can act in a racist and classist way, together with the knowledge that some of their parents had suffered the sharp end of discrimination in employment, and their recognition of the appalling stereotypes on T.V. of Asian, Irish and African people were considered together to build up a picture of Britain as a racist society. The students were able to reflect on these experiences and support each other in understanding the racism implicit in them.

These personal experiences were collected together in a brief sketch which they acted out to help the younger children to think about their own understanding of racism. The sketch and an excerpt from the discussion is featured in the ALTARF video *Race in the Classroom.* The visits the sixth formers made to third and fourth year primary school students were extremely useful. The children appreciated being able to talk in small groups with older girls without the authority figure of of the teacher around. Quite naturally, the subject of sexism also cropped up and it was good for the boys to have older girls there to encourage the girls to discuss this. The sixth form students appreciated the frequently mature assessments of experiences that the primary students were able to make and this encouraged them in their future meetings with younger secondary students.

Challenging Racism in Schools – The Need to Communicate

It all started when sixth form 'afternoons' were introduced to our timetables to provide us with an opportunity for careers advice and for discussing extra-curricular topics. The sessions took the form of films and talks and focused in the first term on 'Race'. Looking back, we can see that the issues raised (in particular – racism) should never have been 'extra-curricular' but should have been an integral part of the whole school curriculum.

One of the first topics we discussed was our experience of racism both in and out of school. This raised the point that racism should be more openly discussed, especially in primary schools. We saw a film about the apartheid system in South Africa, *Last Grave at Dimbaza* and talked about our feelings on it afterwards. For convenience, we split into groups with one or two tutors per group. Towards the end of the afternoon the groups came together to share the outcome of their separate discussions. While some girls were clearly enthusiastic about the discussions, others were trying hard to stifle their yawns and it was evident they would rather have been outside the school gates than within!

However, those of us who felt strongly about racism decided to form a multi-cultural study group in which we could look deeper into the issues of racism and start to tackle the problems involved. At our first meeting we talked about the areas in which we thought we could work. We came to the conclusion that there seemed to be little or no opportunity in our school for issues of race to be discussed within the curriculum. We felt that one way of raising the awareness of students and staff was for us to be involved in the planning of assemblies where we could put our ideas forward. We also came up with the idea of a questionnaire for the students, but that was never formulated, but we did manage to take two assemblies.

The first assembly was intended to be an introduction to the issue of racism for the whole school, and to introduce ourselves as school students who had decided to do something about it. It included dramatic sketches of our experiences of prejudice, and it also criticised racist jokes so often heard on television. We felt that the assembly went down well, but that the upper school were more aware of the problems than the lower school. Some of the younger girls did not seem to have recognised them, or were either surprised or confused because racism had never been talked of in this way before, that is, forced out into the open. We hoped to right the situation before we left the school.

One of the members of our study group was also on the school's multi-cultural working party which was mostly made up of teachers. The working party had just drawn up a letter for parents stating the school's policy on opposing racism. The second assembly our study group organised was designed to introduce this letter. In the assembly we read out speeches by Haile Selassie and Martin Luther King. The same day the letter was given out to the children. The response to both the letter and the assembly was generally quite encouraging but there were a few negative responses to the open statements against racism, as had been expected.

The study group felt that one of the reasons for the lack of awareness of institutional racism in particular, was the lack of discussion about it which we thought should have begun at an early age. We were therefore pleased when the chance came to speak to some primary school children about racial stereotyping. The school was a nearby Junior School where an ex-teacher of our school now taught. The children (10–11 years old) had already discussed racism and their minds were therefore open to ideas we were about to put forward. We performed the sketches from our first assembly and then there was a discussion about them afterwards. The children were eager and responsive, and they felt the afternoon was very rewarding. We followed this up by going back to make a video using some of the ideas from the first discussion.

This work with a local Junior School was near the end of the school year. The coming year was to bring changes which were to affect the study group greatly. Firstly, the teacher who had most helped with the formation of the study group was moved to the lower school (about 7 minutes walk from the site of the upper school) and the sixth form afternoons were renamed 'extension study afternoons'. Sixth formers were now offered a choice of sports instead of the weekly discussions! We still tried to hold discussions on Mondays after school to draw in the lower sixth since some members of the group had now left, and it was getting smaller. But we found that people were not always willing to stay. They were tired after their strenuous exercise and wanted to get home. It became increasingly difficult to hold study group meetings and therefore we could not do as many things as we would have liked.

The major activity of the group in its second year was centred around the making of the Open Door programme *Racism, the 4th R* (available from ALTARF).

School Student Supporters of ALTARF

H. Nemar, Caribbean Times

However, since this was finished there has been anxiety about the continuation of the study group. Will the sixth formers coming up have the same opportunity for discussion and consciousness-raising as we did? How will they become more aware of the issues of race? Unfortunately, we found there were also negative responses to the study group. For example, it was implied by some teachers that certain members of the multi-cultural study group were neglecting their studies because of their involvement with the group. Also, because pupils began to question the content of lessons, teachers began to feel that there was a rise in the number of racist incidents in the school. What they failed to realise was that at long last children were beginning to ask 'Why?' – and surely this is an integral part of learning?

TEACHING ABOUT RACISM IN SOCIAL STUDIES IN NEWHAM

I Aronovsky and *C Sikorski*

The authors are a community education worker and a community worker.

Newham is an East End London Borough with a history of economic instability, low wages, bad housing, massive industrial expansion and decline in the space of 100 years, high immigration throughout its history, and population decline. Despite its honourable place in the history of the Trade Union and Labour movement, it has a continuing record of racism and racist violence, and significant pockets of NF support in the predominantly white dockland areas. Racist violence in Newham has become well known nationally with the murder of Ali Baig in East Ham in 1980, and the recent trial of the Newham Eight. The main perpetrators of racist violence are young people.

The LEA itself has only recently accepted the notion of 'multi-cultural' education, and has yet to formulate clear anti-racist policies or devote resources to developing anti-racist education. It lacks the resources of an authority like ILEA.

Through running a community programme which explored racism amongst other topics with groups of fourth year social studies students, and in common with other concerned teachers, we became aware of the normality of unquestioned racist attitudes and assumptions amongst white school students in Newham. Teachers felt there were no recources available to tackle the issue in the curriculum: they did not want to ignore or avoid the problems of racist views expressed in the classroom, but responding to them without resources and structure often led to polarisation and could merely harden attitudes.

We therefore devised and piloted an extended course on racism with two social studies teachers in 1981. It was used effectively in a predominantly white working-class school with a Docklands catchment, and with stunning success in a multi-racial school. With the agreement of an adviser, we revised the course and launched it in pack form at a conference attended by most social studies departments in the borough.

Most schools in the borough have now used the materials, and some have incorporated them in the syllabus. Even with "ready" materials, taking up the issues of racism in schools where most pupils are white is difficult, and latterly we have concentrated on working with teachers using the course in such schools.

The course is in twelve units with worksheets, questions and back-up information. It begins with a cross cultural simulation game, and is structured around three films – 'Why Prejudice?' BBC TV and two of the 'Our People' series from Thames. Local information and newspaper cuttings are an important feature.

AIMS AND CONTENT

The course explores prejudice and racism in order to create an understanding of why they occur, change attitudes and encourage young people to oppose racism themselves. More specifically the aims are:

1. To look at prejudice and stereotyping relating them to Britain's Imperialist history and to understand the racist and class structure of Britain in the context of imperialism and neo-colonialism.

2. To learn why Asian and Afro-Caribbean people have settled in Britain and in Newham.

3. To expose commonly held racist myths about immigration, employment, housing, education and crime.

4. To examine the facts and consequences of racial discrimination nationally and locally in all these areas today.
5. To create an understanding of the reasons for housing inequality and unemployment in Newham.
6. To show the history and contribution of Black people in Britain.
7. To look at the history of prejudice to immigrant groups in the East End, and to relate this to racism, racial harrassment and violence in Newham today. To put the history of prejudice in the context of the growth of fascism in 20th century Europe and to show what its consequences were and are.
8. To look at contemporary anti-racist struggles and their implications for black and white youths in Britain.

Most groups taking the course have filled in questionnaires at the end designed to find out whether students feel their views have changed, how much information they have retained and their general opinions on the topic.

THE RESULTS IN MULTI-RACIAL SCHOOLS

Particularly where teachers have been relaxed enough or confident to allow open-ended and, therefore, inevitably controversial discussion the results have been very successful. The views and experience of black students expressed openly have been important in changing the attitudes of white classmates.

Q: Have you enjoyed this course?

A: It's enjoyable, you can give your own opinion and listen to other people's opinion and question them. (Black student)

A: Yes, several reasons – one being that I've learnt how other people in the class feel about things compared with myself. (White student)

In practice, bringing the issue of racism out into the open has not been divisive. There have been high levels of participation and 'politically aware' discussions.

Q: Do you think this subject should be taught to other groups? What should be included or left out? Is there anything else you would have liked to discuss?

A: Yes . . . in the other schools – include how and why riots break out. What is being done to keep kids off the streets. I would like to have discussed why the government doesn't help unemployed people instead of building nuclear weapons. (Black student)

NB Quotes from Pilot group, mixed ability, one third Asian, one third Afro-Caribbean, one third white. 1981.

The explanation of an solution to racism is not just located in the prejudices of white individuals. Racism raises fundamental questions about the political economic and social structure of Britain, and the world. The potential for follow-up is limitless. At a more practical level using such a course could be a way of challenging racism within schools, and a stimulus for demanding anti-racist activity and campaigning within schools and in the community.

THE RESULTS IN PREDOMINANTLY WHITE SCHOOLS

Since 1981the course has been used in two schools with a predominantly white catchment and in one multiracial school, in a class with only four black students.

School A:
This school has a good academic reputation. Its catchment is lower middle to working class, from an area adjacent to Docklands. Many students were from owner occupier households. The course was run simultaneously by two teachers with support from us. The head of department was not involved and showed no interest. The teachers told us that racist abuse was common, and that the school had yet to take up the issue. There were no 'working parties' and racist graffitti around the school boundary was a permanent fixture.

The overwhelming ethos in the classes was racist and therefore the process of working through all the issues in detail was emotionally demanding and could feel negative. In this school the reaction by white students was often a bland acceptance of racism as a normal feature of life that could be tolerated, and it was sometimes hard to show why the issue affects white people's lives. This contrasted with the more 'worked up' racism of students from schools in Docklands. We discovered that one of the problems with the groups was little knowledge of 20th century history. Another was a perception of class as a matter of social status, not economic position. This made it difficult to interest the pupils in topics such as the rise of fascism in pre-war Europe, or in housing inequality. A small minority of white students proved to be extremely racist. They usually complied with doing the 'work', but on two occasions could not contain themselves. They said that the contents were all lies and the teacher was trying to brainwash them. Racist letters of complaint came from their parents. These girls were neither supported nor opposed by their classmates. They showed no change of attitude, although in their questionnaire one wrote, "I think Hitler should not have been brought into this course as we should be forgetting him, not remembering what he done".

However, the course was received positively by the

rest of the white students. The response of 17 out of 21 to open-ended questions on what they thought they had learnt showed that they perceived themselves as less prejudiced and felt that their views had changed as a result of the course. Their answers all included comments that black people were not the cause of unemployment and other social problems:

"My views have changed in the way that they don't take our jobs, and I used to think that they did all the muggings, but now I know they don't."

More personally some commented, "I have realised that they have got feelings like us and that they have a hard time in this country."

There were still areas of confusion, but the experience showed what further work needed to be done, and in what way the curriculum could be changed. The black students in the groups were in an uncomfortable position and their comments reflected this. They did not take part in the discussion.

Answers of 1 Asian pupil in one class:–

Q: Which part of the course did you find most interesting?

A: I found this part of the course interesting, where the truth was given. Like we are not responsible for unemployment.

Q: Your own views on discrimination:

A: I think all Blacks and Asians get discrimination from Whites. Especially at school we get picked on by Whites. We get racial attacks and the teachers get abused by older pupils.

Q: Should the course be taught to other classes?

A: Yes and No. If this course has to be taught, the white peopie shouldn't say things against them because that causes arguments and this course can teach people the truth.

These responses indicate the pressures upon black students in such schools. In general, the teachers were pleased with the results and felt that they had gained confidence and developed their own understanding of racism. The course showed concrete ways of re-examining the curriculum on an anti-racist basis. However, the problem at this school was that the teachers were working in isolation. Departments did not communicate formally, and there was no commitment to change, certainly not from the Head.

School B:
The school has a catchment from the heart of working class Docklands. The course was used by the whole department with half the fourth year. The results were encouraging, but there was not time to get through all the materials, nor to have proper assessment meetings. However, there was a commitment to look at the course in relation to what was being done in other departments, and the school was working on anti-racist policies.

School C:
This school's catchment is from Canning Town which is one of the most racist areas in the Borough. One quarter of the school students are black. The course was piloted by the Head of Social Education in a class with four black students. The class is 'low ability' and the materials had to be adapted. There were problems of poor concentration, general lack of interest in school, and lack of confidence in discussion, but nevertheless the results were good. The group seemed on the whole less racist than to start with.

It proved possible to get the pupils to understand the more difficult concepts such as Imperialism by, for instance, stopping the film on it for frequent explanation. A specific lesson to explain the concept of class was included. This enabled the students to see a connection between class and racism.

Q: Do you think the British Empire was a good thing for countries like Africa, India and the West Indies? Give your reason.

A: It was bad, they could not control their own land.

A: They couldn't eat the things or use the things they sent to Britain.

Q: Should this course be taught to other classes?

A: Yes, but when the kids are younger, this will stop the NF and other groups.

Q: What are the reasons for unemployment in Newham?

A: The reason is MAGGIE. She don't care about people who are 1st black . . . 2nd working class . . . 3rd Maggie thinks people are all rich but all people are not. (White students)

The teacher at this school is involving other humanities departments in looking at the materials, and hopes to plan an integrated course whereby departments would teach the topics most relevant to their own subject. In fact the contents straddle all subjects, and the fact that the course has been used mostly by social studies departments has been fortuitous. The potential for developing anti-racist curriculum in this school is good.

CONCLUSIONS

The experience shows that a slot which tackles racism specifically needs preparation and follow-up, and it indicates what these areas of study should be. Using the course reveals the ethno-centrism of the current curriculum.

Committed and concerned teachers can take the issue up, even in an authority not renowned for its progressive stance on these issues. Both within schools and the authority using such a course is a stimulus for developing anti-racist curriculum and policies, gives concrete evidence of the needs and shows the positive case for so doing.

A Newham Housing Estate *North Paddington Community Darkroom*

This is not to underestimate the controversy caused amongst teachers by introducing specific anti-racist materials. The issue can be threatening and promoting such a course can be seen as a criticism of the school and teachers. Two teachers from the pilot schools who were not originally involved have blocked the subsequent use of the materials. However, experience shows that anti-racist education can work, and also that teachers need the resources, facilities and support services.

Anti-racist education questions the whole basis of the existing curriculum, and calls for a massive re-examination of values taken for granted until very recently. Teachers therefore deserve the maximum support and encouragement.

Finally, the experience shows how positive and exciting anti-racist education can be.

Note: For more detailed information about the materials and the results contact ALTARF.

SOCIAL EDUCATION SESSIONS ON THE POLICE, IMMIGRATION AND NATIONALITY

Barbara Bleiman

Social Education is part of the curriculum of all students at Quintin Kynaston. Because it goes beyond the confines of subject boundaries and sees its main function as developing students' ability to arrive at informed judgements on issues in the world around them, it often raises questions related to race and politics.

What follows is a descriptive account of our attempts to discuss two such questions with the Sixth Form, the question of 'The Police and their Role in Society' and the question of 'Immigration and Nationality'. Both issues arose out of events taking place at the time. Sessions on the 'Police' were inserted into the Sixth Form programme soon after the events in Brixton, Toxteth and elsewhere. Likewise, with the introduction of the Nationality Bill, we felt the urgency of informing students of the implications, providing help and advice and discussing the more general issues of immigration law, citizenship and nationality.

THE POLICE AND THEIR ROLE IN SOCIETY

Before describing the final approach adopted, it is worth saying something about the process of arriving at it. There were lengthy and not always easy discussions about how to tackle the issue, with opinion ranging from those who felt that the issue would stir up trouble, those who wanted it to be tackled but felt that the Police should be invited to make their case, to those who firmly opposed the presence of the Police in school. Tutors involved in teaching the Sixth Form, the Headteacher and the Anti-Racist Multicultural Working Party were all involved in discussions at different points. Some students were also involved.

It was finally agreed to base the sessions around work that we prepared ourselves, with considerable help from the local Law Centre, who attended the sessions as well as planning them with us. We agreed not to have a Police presence, although we made it clear to students and other teachers that we would not be presenting just 'one view' of the Police but would try to encourage debate, based on the students' own experiences and the presentation of a full range of different attitudes to policing, from that of the different political parties to the Police Federation or local Community groups. In this way, we hoped to encourage open debate, of a very different kind to the 'short talk, question and answer' approach often used by the Police when they come into schools. The focus on students' own experience of the Police, was an important entry into the discussion and was the basis on which more general issues about policing could be raised.

There were two sessions. Session One focused on students' own experiences and outlined their basic rights. It consisted of:

(a) **Small group discussions based on a ten minute audio tape.**

The tape was made up of descriptions of students' experiences with the Police in a range of different contexts. The students were all at QK, of different ages, and with differing attitudes to the Police. Each discussion group had the following questions, as ideas for discussion:

(1) Have you had similar experiences to those expressed on the tape?

(2) Listen back to the tape.

What would it have been useful for each of these people to know in terms of their rights? (The local Law Centre provided teachers with a list of rights to go with each of the cases on tape.)

(3) Have you come across cases where these rights have been denied?

(4) If so, what could be done about this?

(5) Should individuals have more/less rights in terms of arrest procedures, questioning etc? If so, what?

(b) **A whole group report back from each group**

(c) Again, in the whole group, a summary of the conclusions by the workers from the local Law Centre. The distribution of the Law Centre's information leaflet on young people's rights.

(d) **A display** put on by the local Law Centre.

Session Two looked at more general issues about 'Policing in Society':

(a) **An introduction to the issue**, done by a group of students reading out a variety of statements about policing, taken from newspapers and documents. They ranged from Jim Jardine, Willie Whitelaw, Margaret Thatcher, to local residents, shopkeepers, community representatives, Labour councillors, school students, etc. There were extracts which showed the divisions within the Police Force itself, with statements supporting community policing contrasted with those calling for stronger measures. **A display** of newspaper articles, photographs and quotes was put up.

(b) **Discussions in groups of 10–15**
Each group tackled a slightly different area, so that report-backs to the whole group were varied. The guidelines for each of the discussions were as follows:

Group 1

Do the Police need stronger powers:

To arrest indiviuals?

To deal with civil disorder?

To deal with marches?

To hold people without trial?

Group 2

Could there be a Police Force that is known and respected in the Community?

Think about this in the light of your own experience and views, and in the light of events in Brixton, Southall, Liverpool, at football matches in the community etc.

Group 3

Should the Police be policed?

Is it done now? By whom?

Should the Police be controlled? If so, by whom? If not, why not?

Who should deal with complaints or enquiries into the Police role?

Group 4

Does Society need a Police Force?

If so, for what? If not, why not?

Could other agencies perform any of the roles the Police perform now?

Would that be desirable?

Should the Police perform more roles than they do now?

Group 5

Recent events seem to suggest that tensions between the Police and the community have been heightened.

Do you think this is true?

If so, why and what could be done about it?

Group 6

Should the Police *follow* the Law or should they *make* the Law?

Who should the lawmakers in society be? Judges? Police? Parliament? The local Community?

(c) **Report-backs on discussion groups** to the whole Sixth Form.

The positive aspects of these sessions were that students were able to look at three aspects of policing; first, their own experience; second, their rights in relation to the police and third, the wider issues of the role of the police in society. Starting with their own experiences was important and incidentally told us, as teachers, quite a lot about relations between the Police and our students.

The format of asking students to think through the issues for themselves was valuable but we might have benefitted from the students and teachers having a greater knowledge of the law, upon which to base the detailed discussion of what was fair and unfair and what should be changed. Given the anxieties about raising such a 'controversial' issue with students, we did not feel that our approach had caused problems but rather aired anxieties and issues in a constructive way.

NATIONALITY AND IMMIGRATION

The whole school undertook a project, with the assistance of the local Law Centre, to provide both students and their parents with information and advice about the Nationality Bill. Assemblies and discussions were held for every year in the school, surgeries were set up in the evening and there was a stall at the Summer Fair. It was in this context that the Sixth Form discussed the issue.

With the Sixth Form we decided to look more generally at questions of immigration and nationality as well as giving information about the Nationality Bill. As with the Police, we devoted two one-hour sessions to it.

In *Session One*, we felt that it was important to challenge students' preconceptions and prejudices about immigration. Many had the idea that there were no immigration laws at all and were unaware of the different regulations for EEC citizens, patrials etc. We showed a video about the struggle of Nasira Begum to prove her parentage of her two children in order that they should be able to live with her in Britain. The rest of the session involved small group discussion of the film and the injustices of the present immigration laws that it showed.

Some groups made a start on the second activity which continued into *Session Two*.

The Law Centre produced some hypothetical situations, of would-be immigrants or people living in Britain who wanted a relative or spouse to join them. Students were asked to discuss each of the cases and decide which they thought should be allowed to enter. Existing laws were not discussed or taken into account, just the relative merits of the cases in an ideal world. This led to quite lively debate on the whole notion of immigration restriction. (See end of chapter for cases used.)

Students were then told what would happen to each of these cases under the new Nationality Act and were given a brief resume of its restrictions. (See end of chapter for details.) There was lengthy discussion of the rights and wrongs of the Act, in relation to the students' previous more abstract discussion of what would be 'fair' in each of the cases. As a result of this discussion, students were encouraged to consider what they thought Britain's immigration policy should be.

The sessions generated a lot of interest among

students. Starting with an individual's struggle helped to personalise the issue and also to dispel myths and prejudices. Encouraging the students to think in the abstract about what was 'fair' seemed to give them a framework in which to place the Nationality Act. They could see whether it matched their notion of 'fairness'.

Some students who had direct experience of the immigration laws found the information and surgeries useful and welcomed the chance to debate the issues. However, inevitably, in some groups students did express their prejudices in the course of debate and not all students welcomed the spotlight being turned on immigration. Where students felt confident enough to talk about the problems their families or friends faced in dealing with immigration laws, it was highly revealing for other students. In the main, they felt that the debate was a constructive one.

CONCLUSION

The general conclusions to emerge from our work on the Police and on Nationality and Immigration are that it is possible to deal with the issues in a serious manner with students and that teachers' fears of bringing such issues to the surface are not justified if they are sufficiently carefully presented.

We were very aware, not only that we had to make room for open debate and the airing of a range of different opinions but also that our raising of the issues might be a cause of anxiety to the very students who were most subject to prejudice and discrimination. We actively sought materials and ideas which would avoid stereotyping, sweeping generalisations and misinformation of the kind which is often well intentioned but inaccurate and therefore offensive.

I do feel that these sessions were a qualified success and that schools have a duty to put their energies into making explicit and developing students' understanding of issues, which are so crucial to the students themselves and to our present and future societies.

A RIGHT TO ENTER?

1. Rashid would like to bring his widowed mother from India to join him in London. She has money to support herself there but is emotionally dependent on him since her husband died and has been depressed for some time.
2. Baqua's father is a widower aged 60. He cannot work and has no close relatives in Bangladesh where he now lives. She would like him to live with her in Leeds.
3. Michelle is French and living and working in London. Her parents in Paris are having marital problems. Her mother would like to spend some time in London with her.
4. Klaus is German and is working in London. His rich grandfather loves Harrods. Klaus would like him to come and live with him because he knows that he will shower him with expensive presents.
5. Femi is Nigerian and has been living in Liverpool for many years. His 20-year-old son in Nigeria has just lost his job and Femi has been supporting him. He feels that he might as well support him in Liverpool where he can help him with his business.
6. Mariolyn's 20-year-old daughter in Holland is a student. She would like to take a year off and live with Mariolyn in London where on a visit she recently fell in love with a rockabilly musician.
7. Basha is a Polish doctor working with a work permit in a hospital in Southampton for a year. She would like her husband to join her.
8. Alain is a Belgian working in a law centre. He would like his wife and 10 children to join him.
9. David is a Trinidadian and has lived in London for many years. He has six grandchildren in Trinidad and would like to bring them each over for a year in an English primary school.
10. Zarina, is a British citizen who has been living in Britain since she was 6 months old. She was born in India when her parents were on holiday there. They've lived in London since 1948. Her father fought in the war. On holiday in in India she met a man and wants to marry him and bring him back to Britain with her.
11. Andrea is a shorthand typist who is Italian. She has worked in England for two weeks. She has just married a Pakistani student and wishes to have him live here with her.
12. Rita is separated from her husband. Her son has been living with her husband in Jamaica and her husband has remarried. Her son is extremely unhappy and complains that his stepmother beats him. Rita wants him to join her in England.

Continued . . .

TWELVE PEOPLE WISH TO ENTER THIS COUNTRY. THEY ALL WISH TO ENTER AS DEPENDENTS. YOU, AS A GROUP, ARE RESPONSIBLE FOR MAKING THE DECISION AS TO WHICH SHOULD BE ALLOWED TO ENTER:

1. Discuss the cases and try to come to a group decision.

2. Following on from your discussion and decision, what immigration laws would you suggest for this country?
(You might suggest the basis on which you think dependents should be admitted or refused admission.)

3. Now look at what would actually happen to these people, under the existing laws.
How do the existing laws match up to your proposals?

IF YOU ARE A UK CITIZEN OR SETTLED IN UK:	IF YOU ARE AN EEC NATIONAL:
<u>**Children**</u> must be under 18 *and* have both parents in UK *or* prove that UK parent has sole responsibility *or* prove that other parent is physically or mentally incapable *and* obtain prior Entry Certificate, which can take several years.	<u>**Children**</u> under 21 can walk in
<u>**Parents/Grandparents**</u> can come if widowed mothers, widowed fathers over 65, if both parents travel, one is 65+ *and* they must be wholly or mainly dependent on you *and* prove there are no 'close' relatives able to look after them *and* you can prove you are able to maintain and accommodate them fully. If they are under 65, in *exceptional* circumstances, they may be let in if you can prove that their standard of living is 'substantially' below average in their country, *but* they must obtain prior Entry Certificate.	<u>**Parents/Grandparents**</u> can walk in
<u>**Husbands**</u> *can come in only if wife* is UK born, or has UK born parent *and* both parties have met (that is, not an arranged marriage) *and* husband has obtained prior Entry Certificate. Then he can come in for 12 months initially.	<u>**Husbands**</u> can walk in
<u>**Wives**</u> can walk in (with Entry Cert.)	<u>**Wives**</u> can walk in

Continued . . .

1. Rashid's mother cannot come in; she is not wholly dependant on him.

2. Baqua's father may be destitute, but his standard of living is not 'substantially below' average in Bangladesh.

3. Michelle's mother can come in.

4. Klaus' father can come in for as long as he likes.

5. Femi – His son is too old to come in.

6. Mariolyn's daughter can come in.

7. Basha's husband cannot come and live with her. But a man with a work permit can have his wife come in with him.

8. Alain's wife and children can come in; so could his grand-parents and grandchildren.

9. David's grandchildren can't come in.

10. Zarina was not born here; her husband cannot come and live with her.

11. Andrea's husband can come in (she is an EEC National).

12. Because Rita's son has always been her husband's responsibility, her son cannot join her, no matter how unhappy he is.

Quintin Kynaston School Students *Maeve Dorrian*

QUINTIN KYNASTON SCHOOL

Liz Lindsay

1. Formation of the Working Party 1978

As early as 1977, Peter Newsam, then ILEA Education Officer, issued to all schools a document on Multi-Education. The year 1978 saw the growth of organised overt racist activities in the community with the government immigration laws giving a certain respectability to racist prejudices, which were also becoming more evident within the school.

Protest movements such as ALTARF which, in March 1978, organised a rally attended by 2,000 people, were formed to counteract racism and in 1978 a small multicultural anti-racist working party (MCARWP) was set up at Quintin Kynaston School and was invited to present to the staff a paper summarising the Newsam document and attempting to make the staff more aware of the presence of and the reasons for racist attitudes. The small working party has continued to report the results of their research to staff meetings, has produced documents and initiated discussions on its numerous recommendations and has attempted to increase staff awareness with respect to issues such as:

- i political, economic origins of racist attitudes which result from ignorance and prejudice
- ii evidence of, and methods of dealing with, racist behaviour *within* the school
- iii liaison with parent and community groups
- iv the continued development of an anti-racist curriculum
- v surveys to establish the linguistic diversity of the

students at Quintin Kynaston School and their needs as bilingual students.

Recommendations of the working party accepted by the staff have been gradually incorporated into school policy, so that decisions are seen as the responsibility of *all* staff and not a few individuals.

By 1980, with greatly increasing unemployment figures and economic gloom, fascist groups, especially the B.M. gained greater support from students and there was an increase in graffiti and racial abuse in the school.

2. Adoption of Quintin Kynaston Policy on Racist Behaviour, 1980

In September 1980, the working party presented to a staff meeting an outline of a suggested school policy on racist behaviour, stressing that any successful policy required strong support from the hierarchy and a consistent approach by *all* staff to specific racist incidents. Appropriate school responses were outlined clearly to a checklist of racist offences. The working party recommendations were accepted by the staff and incorporated into the school handbook.

The effectiveness of the school policy on racist behaviour has been monitored by the working party. There appears to be a greater confidence by teachers and students to tackle any racist incidents, which have decreased inside the school. However, attitudes of the 'hard core racists' have probably changed little and their activities may now be confined to activities outside the school. This seemed to be confirmed by the number of Quintin Kynaston students who took part in a B.M. march through the Paddington area in late 1980. On this occasion, the school made its opposition to the B.M. very clear in social education and assemblies and by letters to parents and the local press.

3. Programme to Change Attitudes

The working party has always stressed that the most important need is to change racist attitudes held not only by the extreme neo-fascist groups but unconsciously by the vast majority, who fail to recognise examples of racism and who may behave unintentionally in a racist manner.

Programmes which assist students to explore the full social and economic (as well as moral) implications of racist issues are urgently required. Any general programme must do more than 'teach respect' for other groups by moralising or by examing their cultures and must involve research and participation by students themselves, so that students can understand the political and economic basis of racist ideas as well as of the more blatant neo-fascist activities.

4. ESL Provision at Quintin Kynaston

The Quintin Kynaston intake began to change by 1979 as a result of the primary school link scheme, resulting in an increase in the number of students with a mother tongue other than English (ESL) and a decrease in the number of Afro-Caribbean students.

A survey carried out by the W.P. in 1981 established that 100 students must be classified as ESL students with 43 different mother tongue languages. With the help of the Netley Language Centre, a document was prepared by the working party on the implications of presence of ESL students.

The W.P. stressed the need for at least one full-time ESL teacher on-site, to support students in the mainstream classroom and to advise teachers. The set-up of ESL students travelling to a language centre was considered unsatisfactory socially as there was little interaction with English-speaking students and also it was unproductive not to learn English language in a context where learners are required to use the English language for a particular purpose.

Early in 1981, Quintin Kynaston was extremely fortunate to have John Wright appointed as 0.5 teacher funded by INSET to research the school's needs to develop some appropriate material for incorporation into school policy programmes. With co-operation from the working party, he produced some excellent documents containing a great amount of not readily accessible information and guidelines for teachers and gave guidelines for teachers and tutors for class discussions. He also initiated work on ESL classes and set up a Cantonese class.

John assisted the W.P. in its strong recommendations for an ESL teacher. In September 1981, Quintin Kynaston obtained its first full-time ESL teacher on-site. Last year, an ESL teacher was appointed and despite very poor accommodation he has greatly assisted the introduction and integration of the new ESL students into school life and has greatly increased their confidence and their ability to learn. At the same time, we feel the school should review and ask for more resources for extra ESL teachers and for some main-stream teachers to be time-tabled to prepare materials.

5. Liaison with Parents and Community

Parents are made fully aware that Quintin Kynaston, a comprehensive school respecting all students of equal value and importance, is intolerant of racist behaviour and aims to provide a secure environment where all students are free to learn. Leaflets are distributed at a stall at Quintin Kynaston annual fairs and surgeries are set up at some parent-teacher nights where specialists from West Hampstead Law Centre are present to provide on request information and advice to families e.g. regarding the recently introduced Nationality Act.

The working party considers that the school should gain sufficient credibility with the community on its anti-racist stance, so that families gain enough confidence to report to the school any harassment suffered from racist groups.

Links have been established with the Camden CCR Racial Harassment Monitoring Group because one of the Quintin Kynaston students was identified as being a member of a gang harassing a Bengali family. Some members of the working party also serve on the Camden CCR Education sub-committee.

6. In-Service Conferences

In order to increase staff awareness and understanding of the racism experienced by students in the community, the working party organised a conference for Division 2 teachers. Workshops were led by members of the Law Centre, Camden CCR and the CRE. This was later followed by a conference on anti-racist strategies in the classroom. The response to both conferences was positive and we hope to organise further conferences as requested by the participants using INSET funds.

7. Student Involvement

During the past 12 months, Quintin Kynaston students and the students' council have become increasingly involved in monitoring the effectiveness of, and helping to implement, the Quintin Kynaston anti-racist policy. Their interest was stimulated by their active participation at the end of 1982 in the production of ALTARF's BBC Open Door Programme *Racism . . . the 4th R*, students writing scripts and interviewing the Quintin Kynaston head, Peter Mitchell, regarding the school policy and also Azim Hajee, from the West Hampstead Law Centre, regarding the work of the Centre within the school. Some students were involved in a discussion about the way racist ideas are reinforced by some curricula which they consider should be revised. A poem and artwork by students were also part of the programme.

A video made at the school by a group of upper school students records a discussion by students of their experiences at the school. The W.P. intends to use this video to increase staff awareness of students' experience.

A number of 6th formers and a 5th year student who, as part of her English coursework, researched the effectiveness of the school anti-racist policy, concluded that the existence of the school policy was not made explicit enough, especially to incoming students. After a discussion with the school council, the students and the council have together produced a leaflet, to be issued to all incoming students in the new school year. The leaflet very briefly explains that the school has both an anti-racist and anti-sexist policy and that all students are equally valued. (See page 205)

The leaflet assures new students that the school will support them if any other student attempts to discriminate against them on the grounds of sex or ethnic origin.

Recently, some 6th form students addressed a staff meeting and were critical of the exclusion from the school policy of any mention of possible racist behaviour amongst teachers. The students wanted assurance that if necessary action would be taken against members of staff who behave in a racist manner. They also considered that the school should be explicit on its anti-racist stand not only during interviews with incoming students but also in the recruitment of teachers.

8. Urgent Provision for 1983-1984

While Quintin Kynaston's anti-racist policy (September 1980) has proved reasonably effective with respect to overt and intentional racism, there is an urgent need for further development of resources to attack 'prejudice and ignorance' among both staff and students in which unconscious, unintentional racism thrives. Many original programmes still need to be designed in all subject areas by people who have an awareness, insight and understanding, not only of racism, but also of the school and classes for whom they are developed. Members of the working party have not had the considerable amount of time for research, discussion and production required to develop many of their ideas for appropriate resource material. All teachers are subject to tremendous pressure, with their heavy teaching loads, meetings and extra-curricular activities.

ILEA, in its publication *Anti-Racist Guidelines for Schools and Colleges* (April 1983), stresses the urgent need to encourage students to make an analysis of racism which must take into account economic and power relations, political, historical and cultural factors. Hopefully, the ILEA multi-ethnic staff will soon have prepared for issue to schools original material for all subject areas which will motivate and stimulate students' own research, discovery and discussion in the classroom. Such material can supplement but not replace the type of material best prepared by school working parties, appropriate for the classes for whom they are designed.

Addendum 83-84

QK is by no means complacent about having eradicated racism at the school. Indeed, the further we have extended our investigations the more examples of racism we have found. These have not been of the kind of overt, fascist behaviour, slogans and graffitti evident in 1979-80 but include the incidence of snide comments being made with derogatory, racist overtones and also the continuing existence of the firmly embedded unconscious, racist attitudes of the majority. This evidence has been obtained from separate discussions with both parents and students.

In March 1984, a meeting was jointly organised by the parents and the working party. Members of the working party together with Camden CCR, local Black parents groups and school students made up a panel to answer questions and take part in the discussions after the showing of the ALTARF video *Racism the 4th R.* It is not surprising that the topic generated so much discussion and, in some cases, anger and frustration but it was agreed that the meeting had been one of the most useful for parents for a long time and had made an excellent start on raising consciousness on racism. The parents have formed a parents' group to discuss further issues raised and will be preparing a parents' anti-racist statement.

Students have been active in the last 12 months. Two more videos have been made by senior students and by a group of 2nd years. Student discussions are extremely useful for raising staff/parent awareness of the issues of racism.

A number of students contributed to the School Student issue of the ALTARF Newsletter (No. 8). Their articles were read out to the full staff meeting and made available for parents at QK.

Students will be discussing racism in their forms during Social Education and form representatives will express the feelings of each group to a group of the School Council which will then formulate a students' anti-racist policy. Such open discussion has been encouraged and is further developed by the school as the students become more confident that they can discuss their feelings and attitudes. It is hoped finally to bring together representatives of parents, staff and students to look at and discuss the anti-racist policies of all 3 groups.

In line with the ILEA Anti-Racist statements and Guidelines (October 83) QK, as well as other schools, is trying to prepare anti-racist statements. In 1980, QK developed its anti-racist policy which, in line with ILEA policy, provided:

1. a clear unambiguous statement of opposition to any form of racism or racist behaviour;
2. a firm expression of all pupils' rights to the best possible education; and
3. a clear indication of what is not acceptable and procedures including sanctions to deal with any transgressions.

However, as the ILEA guidelines state it is 'ineffective to tackle avowed racism of growing children and young people without an equal concern with our own ideas and practices'.

The Guidelines also acknowledge that 'we are all in some way racist and must become consciously and rigorously anti-racist'.

'Urgently needed is fuller background resource material of a general nature, detailing examples of structural, political, ideological, historical and cultural factors which are so basic to any analysis and understanding of racism. Preparation of such material could be best done by the ILEA staff appointed and attached to the Inspectorate with responsibility for development of anti-racist strategies, for co-ordination in Divisions and for production of resource materials.' (ILEA October 1983 – *The Authority's initiative on Multi-ethnic Education in Schools*.)

There is very little material on the market adapted to the appropriate level of language and to anti-racist perspectives. Groups of teachers who have already demonstrated their ability to develop such materials should be seconded from various schools to work collectively to produce resources for specific subject areas. Such teachers should be in close contact with and fully aware of the needs and interests of the 90% of the secondary school school population who will not be doing advanced study at a tertiary level. These teachers should therefore be prepared to replace topics which have traditionally formed part of the curriculum and have involved primarily a didactic method and a memorisation of terms and facts. These teachers need to select from the vast amount of knowledge in a particular subject, topics which are relevant to students' needs and interests and which will encourage their active participation and develop their critical and analytical skills. Such a curriculum should provide students with the knowledge and analytical skills necessary for understanding prejudice, discrimination and oppression.

Quintin Kynaston – equal opportunity school

EQUAL OPPORTUNITIES

Q.K. is a COMPREHENSIVE school. That means it is for everybody. In this school, we believe that everyone has a right to equal chances. Sometimes, people get 'put down' because of their colour or their race. Some people still think boys are better than girls. Q.K. school has policies about this.

RACISM

- There are more than 33 languages spoken in Q.K.
- That means our students' families have come from all over the world.
- People at Q.K. are glad that it is a multi-cultural school.
- You'll learn about many different cultures and countries.
- You'll also find out and discuss why people are prejudiced against other people.
- If anyone tries to 'put you down' because of your race or colour, religion, nationality, language or culture, the school will support you.
- Please report any racist comments or behaviour to a teacher or your head of year.

SEXISM

- There are no 'girls'' subjects and 'boys'' subjects. For the first three years, everyone does the same subjects. After that, you choose.
- You'll get lots of advice and help, when it's time to choose. You are encouraged to think about what's best for YOU.
- You'll learn about how people grow up thinking that women are not as good as men. At Q.K., we know that's not true.
- If anyone tries to 'put you down' because of your sex, the school will support you.
- Please report any sexist comments or behaviour to a teacher, or your head of year.

OUR SCHOOL COUNCIL

Q.K. has a school council where people with complaints or ideas can be heard.
If you want to work against racism or sexism, join your year Council.

REMEMBER

Nobody is better than anybody else. Treat everyone with the same respect as you expect for yourself.

Children Protest at Friends' Deportation

Anna Sherwin

ANTI-RACIST POLICIES

Laurie Lax

Over the past ten or more years the concept of multi-cultural education has been a central focus of attention for many researchers and has become a more common if still far from universal practice in our schools. A growing number of LEAs have formulated policies for the education of young people growing up in a multi-cultural society. Such policies acknowledge the cultural diversity of school and community emphasising its potential as a teaching and learning resource. Accompanying objectives of this sort is the recognition – variously stated – of the racist nature of contemporary British society and the need for schools to play their part in combatting racism.

The inadequacy for such a task of a multi-cultural approach which does not examine the political aspects of racism has been emphasised elsewhere in this book (see Anti-racist teaching: General principles). ALTARF recognises also the limitations which arise from the role of school as one of the important instruments through which the prevailing features of a society's dominant cultural system are transmitted. The extent to which anti-racism can become an effective and accepted educational practice within the mainstream schools operating in a fundamentally racist society is clearly limited and serves to remind all anti-racists of the need to be involved in the wider struggle.

In order to maximise the contribution that schools can make to the struggle against racism, ALTARF believes that all schools must prepare and pursue a positive anti-racist policy. We believe that an effective anti-racist policy must be a positive programme concerned with all aspects of school life including the curriculum, organisation and links with the community it serves. It is important that within such a policy there is a standard procedure for dealing with racist behaviour but it would be of limited value if it dealt only with overt racism (more limited still if the code were seen to apply only to pupils).

It is interesting to note, for example, that in the ALTARF video *Racism the 4th R* the then Head of Quintin Kynaston School answered about racist pupils when the interviewer asked how he would deal with racist people. Other school student members of ALTARF have noted the double standards applied in this area to pupils and teachers – pupils are punished, perhaps suspended, for racist remarks or racist behaviour whilst staff go unchallenged. Sometimes pupils challenge teacher racism and are then labelled as 'stroppy'.

Dealing with racism is not simply a matter of enforcing school rules. It must take the form of a whole school policy which looks at both the hidden party and the direct content of the curriculum, the way in which the school is organised and how it relates to the wide community. This kind of all-encompassing approach to anti-racism has some chance of succeeding whereas the superficial response taken up by most schools is more concerned with being *seen* to be doing something rather than *actually* doing anything, (I understand that in the British Army it's known as TGIC – Thank God I'm Covered).

STARTING POINTS

The initiative for discussions about the introduction of an anti-racist policy may come about in a variety of ways. It may come from an individual; arise out of a specific incident; be the result of a collective decision to re-examine books and materials. Increasingly nowadays it may be that the Local Education Authority itself is making some request that the schools take such an initiative, LEAs have a statutory obligation under the 1976 Race Relations Act to 'take positive action to eliminate discrimination and promote equal opportunities, understanding and good race relations between groups in the community'. The extent to which this obligation is reflected in official policies and practices varies considerably – underlining once more the need for anti-racists to be involved in action outside school.

There are at present some 20 or so LEAs which have introduced an anti-racist/multi-cultural policy in schools or, more precisely, on paper. Whilst this development may have made it easier for individuals to raise the subject of anti-racism for discussion in schools, it does not, by any means, guarantee its implementation. In so far as the problem (for those associated with the 20 authorities) now seems to be one of attempting to get a policy implemented rather than one of stating an intervention, this may be seen as 'progress and the fruits of victory'. However, if one looks more closely at the policies and practices of these 20 'progressive' LEAs – the vague commitments; the lack of support given to anti-racists; the way in which Black staff are treated – the alarming gap which appears between County Hall paper and school practice will certainly dispel any thoughts of celebration.

Notwithstanding the realistic reservations expressed above, (and being aware that time may prove that such policies constitute no more than a cynical exercise in political expediency) anti-racists have, in general, welcomed LEA directives on anti-racist education as a qualified opportunity to raise issues and examine practices. The Inner London Education Authority, for example, has reviewed and reinforced its commitment to anti-racist/multi-ethnic education and has requested all its institutions to prepare a carefully thought out anti-racist policy for implementation by late 1984. It is vital that this process of preparing a whole school policy is thorough; that it involves everyone connected with the school and that it does not end up as just another piece of paper in the headteacher's desk. In a similar exercise following the publication of the Bullock Report in 1975, all ILEA schools were instructed to produce a statement on their language policy. They did so but the effect on their school practices was negligible. There is every indication that the current initiatives will suffer a similar fate.

To avoid the production of a meaningless paper policy it is necessary to try to ensure that the preparatory process is thoroughly conducted. Individuals will need to plan their own course of action and devise strategies to suit their own circumstances. Among the most important stages in this process are:

1. Identifying areas of support

It is vital to locate areas of support both within the school community and outside it. This support may include using existing resources in terms of people, structures and materials which are potentially useful. It may take the form of becoming involved in local initiatives; joining anti-racist organisations; attending related meetings and in-service courses; collecting materials and resources to promote discussion and to increase colleagues' awareness of institutional and personal racism.

As a corollary to this strategy of identifying areas of potential support, it is wise also to be aware of areas of likely resistance and to locate potential blockages. In this I would include personal style (how you come across to others); the likely response of senior staff and office holders; the nature and extent of school democracy; being used as the expert who knows all the answers (and who does all the work). The working party approach is obviously better than the individual post holder or 'interested' person being solely responsible for developing anti-racist work. However, this too has drawbacks if their recommendations and findings are automatically agreed without a full discussion of their implications for the school's practices.

Another strategy which may help to ensure thoroughness is to anticipate and plan the most effective response to the most common objections to anti-racist education.

2. Knowing the objections

Many people object to the introduction of an anti-racist programme as irrelevant to primary school children; likely to cause discomfiture to Black pupils and resentment among Whites; too overtly political; damaging to academic standards; likely to stir up trouble where none exists.

It is best to tackle these objections as part of the thorough examination of the issues involved. In attempting to use the opposing arguments as a valuable part of the discussions, it is essential to avoid 'verbal ping-pont' in which each side presents its own pre-packaged case. Beating opponents over the head with ones' argument serves no useful purpose but neither does pretending that no such deep differences exist.

By reference to the existing structures and practices within a school it should be possible for everyone to examine some of the taken-for-granted assumptions which underlie some of the common objections to anti-racism outlined above. Whether this process results in colleagues viewing the introduction of anti-racist work more sympathetically let alone becoming committed to its implementation remains in serious doubt. It certainly hasn't worked that neatly in my experience but it may be helping to shift the balance of opinion and to raise consciousness. The kind of full and open discussions that can take place by a close examination of anxieties and misgivings about such work made in relation to existing school practices may be a useful preparation for the main discussions which constitute the third stage of this long-term progress.

3. Setting the agenda and involving everyone

The whole process of preparing and following a positive anti-racist policy must involve as many people as possible connected with the school. The topics covered must be as wide ranging as possible and collectively agreed at an initial meeting. Governors, parents, pupils, ancillary staff as well as teachers should be involved in planning the programme of discussions. They should be free to organise their own contributions and to express their own views. Pupils themselves have important contributions to make and their views on school policies can be illuminating. Their personal experiences need to be taken more seriously but children's rights in general seem scarcely to exist. School councils involving children in the decision-making process are virtually non-existent too. It is easy to scoff at this sort of recommendation as absurdly impractical but it is in fact easy enough to provide a forum for primary pupils to express their views and relate their experiences.

It is also easy for colleagues to dismiss 'meetings to talk about what we're going to talk about at meetings' as an unnecessary waste of time. But if it makes subsequent meetings more useful and efficient it may be time well spent. It is also more likely to ensure that the discussions cover all the important issues than relying on the skill of the chairperson to keep the discussions on the right lines.

Among the areas which should be included on the agenda are: school policy and objectives; LEA policy; language; resources; organisation; community involvement; curriculum; staff appointments. The theme of racism and anti-racism should run throughout the discussions. This does not mean that a separate series of meetings looking at the nature and extent of racism should not be held as has been done by some schools.

Many colleagues do not accept the analysis of Britain as a racist state with a racist history and racist laws and institutions. They may interpret racism as right-wing extremism or reduce it to a question of personal prejudice. To provide an understanding of the context of racism – its all pervasive nature, its economic, social and historical dimensions – is a tall order and takes the discussions far beyond the normally accepted brief of primary schools. But it is a pre-requisite to ensuring thorough inquiry.

The way in which any discussions are conducted reveals a great deal about the democratic structure of a school. As with the wider society, schools are not as democratic as they claim (although sometimes the pretence can be exploited). Many primary schools of my experience hold regular staff meetings which amount to no more than briefing sessions. They are most often restricted to teaching staff alone (although often the decisions taken affect many others), with very little attempt made to provide a real forum for discussion. There is a tendency for senior staff to dominate the discussion; to ignore the need to speak through the chair (most often occupied by the head rather than on a rotating basis). It is also common practice for heads or senior staff to set the terms for the agenda. The decision making machinery is controlled in most schools by the hierarchy to the exclusion of less senior staff, parents and pupils. Teachers, parents and political members of the governing body can play an independent role but are often content to rubber-stamp any educational proposals.

Such undemocratic practices are inimical to any valuable discussions and should be challenged through the NUT and other channels. This again highlights the long-term aspects of policy-making and the need for extra-school activities.

Setting the agenda and involving everyone is for many schools such a radical departure from standard practice as to be inconceivable. Such schools will no doubt, conduct a sham, superficial, little exercise aimed at fulfilling the minimum conditions of the LEA directive. They may put up a little display of multicultural work and then dismiss as aggressive, those people who find such tokenism insulting and say so. Those schools which have responded to the ILEA initiatives by a conscientious and thorough attempt to review their practices and procedures are few and far between.

The policy document produced at the end of the collectively conducted process should be comprehensive in its range and include not only a positive statement against racism but also details of the curriculum (hidden and formal) school organisation and links with the community. It should then be publicised and made available to everybody connected with the school. Some machinery for ensuring the implementation of the agreed policy, of evaluating and reviewing it should be written into the term of reference.

The capacity of schools to achieve the kind of effective anti-racist policy being advocated here is clearly limited by the relationship between school and society. Nevertheless, it is important to recognise that there are many teachers, pupils and schools whose policies and practices do challenge the dominant values of a racist, sexist and classist society. Those who do not, will be seen as upholding such values.

The process in practice

The following case shows how difficult it is to get a school committee to combatting racism – even where, to some extent, conditions are favourable.

My own experience of contributing to development of an effective whole school policy proved to be a protracted and frustrating process. Initially, conditions obtained in the school seemed conducive to success. It is an ILEA school where several teachers had attended or were attending in-service courses at the Centre for Urban Education Studies, part of the Centre for Education in a Multi-ethnic Society (all had chosen to attend and were apparently sympathetic or committed). Of the remaining teachers only two were positively hostile (one was the Deputy Head) and, most encouraging of all, the Head *seemed* supportive. I did not at this stage know much about the ancillary staff, the parents or the governors – all of whom have an important role to play in the process. Against these potential advantages, some likely obstacles could be clearly perceived (others less so). The school catchment area provided a largely white middle class intake with an emphasis on academic standards achieved via a traditional curriculum. There was little immediate evidence of any overtly racist behaviour from the children (with the exception of a continuing, unresolved and generally ignored feud between a white pupil and his black classmates). Most teachers taught formally, concentrating on basic skills with little or no attention given to mixed ability grouping, collaborative learning or the active participation by pupils in the organisation of their own work. My own position as a temporary teacher committed to anti-racism and using substantially different teaching methods did not provide me with a secure base.

During the first half term I tried to establish my own credentials as a competent class teacher in addition to developing closer working relationships with certain colleagues. I also met parents and governors including some involved in the Anti-Apartheid movement, some who openly stated their anti-racist position and perhaps, the majority who seemed caring but not particularly political. (They were most actively political at a later date when they saw their own interests threatened by the proposed break-up of ILEA. Staff, parents and governors worked together in a successful campaign.)

This school operated a system whereby a teacher leads a discussion on a subject of her/his choice. It is advisable for teachers doing this to prepare and circulate any relevant papers beforehand. A few days before the staff meeting, I distributed copies of ILEA's 1979 Progress Report on Multi-ethnic Education in which ILEA's major objectives are outlined. It was my intention to obtain some kind of commitment to examining school practices in the light of these objectives. My colleagues who were attending related courses at CUES supported my call for a longer staff meeting to be devoted to such an inquiry. At this school there were usually two longer staff meetings a term when the school was closed early and the staff discussed a specific area of the curriculum. It was also agreed that the BBC TV series *Multicultural Education* should be taped and used as a resource for the discussions.

The longer staff meeting took place as planned. It was introduced by the Head as another in a series of meetings looking at areas of the curriculum. This was not the basis on which the meeting had been proposed. To see multi-ethnic education/anti-racism as a separate area of the curriculum constitutes a narrow view rather than an overall perspective and was in this case, a deliberate and successful attempt to restrict the discussions. The TV programme was concerned with the need for a multicultural curriculum in all-white schools (which was pertinent given the school intake) and was generally well received (that is, it was sufficiently moderate to be acceptable to most). The TV programme concentrated on a non-political multicultural approach which attempts to eliminate prejudice in young people (racism wasn't mentioned) by teaching them about other cultures. (A later programme in the series, *Teacher examine Thyself*, did look briefly at institutional racism and the compilation, *Anglo Saxon Attitudes* includes the question of teacher racism and might therefore, be a useful resource for staff discussions.)

The question of racism and the school's response to it received very little attention during these discussions.

When the issue was raised, objections were made on two counts – the overtly political nature of anti-racism and the claimed rarity of racism in the school. Where racism was acknowledged – in terms of racist abuse and graffiti, never school practices or staff attitudes – it was seen as an offence on a par with other misbehaviour adequately covered by the school's existing code.

As the need for a positive anti-racist policy had been ignored, I proposed that there should be another meeting which concentrated on racism and in which we looked thoroughly at school practices and at the kind of objections expressed earlier. This was accepted in principle but no date was fixed. It seemed clear that no such whole school investigation into racism would take place as the senior staff had already decided what would be a safe distance to travel down this particular road.

Analysing the failure of the meeting was a depressing task, particularly in view of the original high hopes. Among the major miscalculations I made was the assumption that those colleagues who seemed sympathetic and committed to anti-racism shared a similar outlook and followed a similar line. Some contested the view of racism as a white problem; others subsumed anti-racist activities under the general struggle against class oppression in a capitalist society (i.e. they did nothing specific).

The ostensibly supportive stance from the head turned out to be a mask to cover containing or obstructive ploys. I had thought that the planned meeting would be the first stage of a collective process aimed at examining school practices in the light of ILEA policy but the long term commitment to such a task was missing. Perhaps ILEA's current initiatives will have encouraged a more thorough examination of school practices and attitudes.

I concentrated my remaining efforts to raise the issue of racism in other ways: through school NUT meetings; informal but specific discussions with certain colleagues; approaches to parents and governors; links with local agencies, such as the CCR and the teachers' centre. All of these were useful though limited sometimes to two or three people. The out of school discussions and activities were especially valuable from the consciousness raising point of view. The definition of racism was followed by racism awareness activities. Justifiable criticism has been levelled at racism awareness programmes which ignore the existence of institutional racism treating racism instead as a psychological problem. However, to ignore the racist attitudes spawned and nourished by societal structures is also an incomplete analysis. Those of us who are white have to confront our own racism and recognising it as conditioning from which we have benefitted materially in the past (and continue to do so today) may be helpful at the beginning of the process. Confronting one's own racism is a painful and threatening process and one which most white teachers continue to resist. Challenging racism must involve challenging its personal as well as its institutional manifestations.

OTHER PUBLICATIONS

Race in the Classroom – The Primary Workshop's first booklet on anti-racist teaching in the primary school. 'I am sure that you will gain from this book and see that it is a step in securing the logical position of good education requiring anti-racist teaching, multi-cultural education and a growing world perspective as part of all that is held important already in primary education.' Bev Woodroffe, ILEA Senior Multi-Ethnic Inspector. 60 pence plus postage and packing.

Teaching and Racism – anti-racist teaching in the secondary school. The Secondary Workshop's first booklet. 60 pence plus postage and packing.

Divide and Rule – Never! – Pupils' support materials to go with the film of the same name, but suitable for use without the film. Includes: Who are 'British People' Anyway?; Immigration: What Are The Facts?; What Was So Great About The British Empire? and lots more. 60 pence plus postage and packing. (Reductions for bulk orders 10 for £5 or 30 for £13.50 plus postage and packing.)

Video – *Racism the 4th R.* This much praised film made by ALTARF for the BBC2 Open Door Programme is available on VHS Cassette from ALTARF. The film shows anti-racist work in primary and secondary schools and includes interviews with parents, pupils and black teachers. Useful for starting off staffroom or PTA discussions on the issues. No charge but donation welcome, plus postage and packing.

All available from ALTARF, Room 216, Panther House, 38 Mount Pleasant, London WC1X 0AP. Tel: 01-278 7856.

ALTARF Membership entitling members to regular mailings and Newsletters is also available. Details from above address.

OTHER PUBLICATIONS

[illegible]

Available from ALTARF, Room 216, Panther House, 38 Mount Pleasant, London WC1X 0AP. Tel: 01-[illegible]

[illegible]